Robert E. Slavin
Olatokunbo S. Fashola

Show Me the Evidence!

Proven and Promising Programs for America's Schools

CORWIN PRESS, INC.
A Sage Publications Company
Thousand Oaks, California

For information:

Corwin Press, Inc.
A Sage Publications Company
2455 Teller Road
Thousand Oaks, California 91320
E-mail: order@corwinpress.com

SAGE Publications Ltd.
6 Bonhill Street
London EC2A 4PU
United Kingdom

SAGE Publications India Pvt. Ltd.
M-32 Market
Greater Kailash I
New Delhi 110 048 India

Printed in the United States of America

Library of Congress Cataloging-in-Publication Data

Slavin, Robert E.
   Show me the evidence! : Proven and promising programs for
America's schools / Robert E. Slavin, Olatokunbo S. Fashola.
      p. cm.
   Includes bibliographical references.
   ISBN 0-8039-6710-1 (cloth : acid-free paper) — ISBN 0-8039-6711-X
(pbk. : acid-free paper)
      1. School improvement programs — United States — Case studies.
   2. Educational innovations — United States — Case studies.
   I. Fashola, Olatokunbo S.   II. Title.
   LB2822.82.S53   1998   97-45273

This book is printed on acid-free paper.

98 99 00 01 02 03 10 9 8 7 6 5 4 3 2

Production Editor: S. Marlene Head
Editorial Assistant: Kristen L. Gibson
Typesetter: Joan Gazdik Gillner
Cover Designer: Marcia M. Rosenburg

Contents

Preface

———◆———

Educators, policymakers, and researchers are constantly bombarded with claims about the effectiveness of various programs and policies intended to improve children's achievement. Every program operating in more than a few schools can point to some school or classroom where "remarkable gains" were seen, at least on some measure in some year. Every program can produce at least one enthusiastic endorsement from a teacher or principal. But what really works? Among the hundreds of classroom or school innovations able to work in schools, which are really likely to improve student achievement, if properly implemented? Finding the answer to this question is often difficult and time consuming, as evaluation evidence may be hard to find and, sometimes, hard to interpret. In particular, it's difficult to compare apples to apples, to evaluate alternative programs against a consistent set of standards. As a result, educators often disregard evidence and make decisions based on what's easy, what's politically palatable, or what's marketed in an appealing way.

This purpose of this book is to change this state of affairs. It presents reviews of programs for elementary and secondary schools that are widely available and have some evidence of effectiveness in terms of student achievement, and discusses district-level strategies for introducing proven programs. We've tried to apply a consistent standard of effectiveness and replicability that is fair to different programs with different research traditions. Our standards strongly emphasize the question any educator most wants to know about a program: If we implement this program as intended, is it likely to increase our students' achievement more than what we're doing now, or more than other alternatives? In other words, we emphasize comparisons of programs to similar control groups, which really represent what the experimental groups would have achieved without the program.

The importance of objective evidence of effectiveness has always been great in evaluating educational programs but has been heightened by several recent developments. For the first time, policymakers are beginning to demand evidence, and to provide funding to schools to adopt programs with evidence of effectiveness. Recently, the U.S. Congress approved a funding plan in which schools could receive funding to help them with the start-up costs of proven whole-school designs. A particular focus of this plan is on encouraging Title I schools to devote their resources to proven programs rather than to traditional uses of these funds, such as pull-out remedial programs and paraprofessionals. Several states, including Ohio, Minnesota, and Louisiana, have passed or are considering legislation that would fund programs with evidence of effectiveness, especially in the area of literacy.

One word of caution: The evidence presented in this book is far from ideal. If we'd applied very stringent standards, this would be a thin volume indeed. We believe it is better to know the "state of the art" with respect to evidence on particular programs, even if this evidence is incomplete or flawed. But the reader should carefully evaluate the evidence presented here. Have program evaluations been replicated? Have they been done by third-party evaluators? Have they taken place in schools like yours?

Beyond helping educators make choices among replicable programs, we hope to contribute to a change in the national conversation about school reform, to move it away from ideological and political considerations toward use of evidence. School reform will never get off of the pendulum swings of current fashion until educators and policymakers demand, "Show me the evidence!"

We also hope this volume will help build support for the creation of new evidence about program outcomes. The current state of knowledge about what works is better than nothing, but far from what it should be. At present, there are few mechanisms for evaluation of replicable programs. Those that do exist are usually carried out by the developers themselves.

Educational innovation lacks the respect for scientific evidence and independent replication that has characterized the most productive and progressive aspects of our society and economy, from medicine, technology, and engineering to agriculture. We know far more about the safety and effectiveness of our children's shampoo than we do about the reading or math programs their teachers use. Our children, our teachers, and our society deserve much better.

This book was written primarily to give educators, evaluators, and researchers the most comprehensive and objective evidence we could locate on programs schools could use to significantly improve student outcomes, as well as suggestions for how school districts might create districtwide strategies for introducing, evaluating, and spreading effective methods over time. The book describes the current state of evidence for replicable programs available to elementary and secondary schools, with a particular focus on programs that are widely known, widely used, and, in principle at least, widely replicable. A special focus of the review is on schoolwide programs capable of being used in Title I schoolwide projects, or in schools receiving funding from the new whole-school reform legislation. However, replicable programs focused on specific subjects or on specific purposes (e.g., dropout prevention or classroom management) are also reviewed, both for their intrinsic merit and for the possibility that schools might create their own paths to whole-school reform by phasing in proven curricular reforms.

The preparation of this book was primarily funded by a grant from the Office of Educational Research and Improvement, U.S. Department of Education (No. R-117D-40005), and some of the material in it began as a set of technical reports for the Hispanic Dropout Project, also funded by the U.S. Department of Education. However, any opinions expressed are those of the authors alone and do not necessarily represent the positions or policies of the U.S. Department of Education or other funders.

About the Authors

Robert E. Slavin is currently Co-Director of the Center for Research on the Education of Students Placed at Risk at Johns Hopkins University. He received his BA in Psychology from Reed College in 1972 and his PhD in Social Relations in 1975 from Johns Hopkins University. Slavin has authored or coauthored more than 180 articles and 15 books, including *Educational Psychology: Theory Into Practice* (Allyn & Bacon, 1986, 1988, 1991, 1994), *School and Classroom Organization* (Erlbaum, 1989), *Effective Programs for Students at Risk* (Allyn & Bacon, 1989), *Cooperative Learning: Theory, Research, and Practice* (Allyn & Bacon, 1990, 1995), *Preventing Early School Failure* (Allyn & Bacon, 1994), and *Every Child, Every School: Success for All* (Corwin, 1996). He received the American Educational Research Association's (AERA) Raymond B. Cattell Early Career Award for Programmatic Research in 1986, the Palmer O. Johnson award for the best article in an AERA journal in 1988, and the Charles A. Dana award in 1994.

Olatokunbo S. Fashola is an Associate Research Scientist at the Johns Hopkins University Center for Research on the Education of Students Placed at Risk. She received her PhD in 1995 from the University of California, Santa Barbara. Her research interests include reading, language development, emergent literacy, program evaluation, educational policy issues, problem solving, and bilingual education.

1

Show Me the Evidence!

◆

In 1983, a blue-ribbon commission issued a ringing call to arms to reform America's schools. Decrying a "rising tide of mediocrity," *A Nation at Risk* (National Commission on Excellence in Education, 1983) proposed sweeping reforms for America's elementary and secondary schools. This and other reports kicked off 15 years of nonstop discussion, debate, and policy making, which is still in full swing today. Recently, President Clinton has declared education a top priority, and he has proposed national tests and volunteer tutoring to help make America's schools the best in the world.

However, the reform movements of the 1980s and 1990s have had little substantive impact on teaching and learning. Scores on the respected National Assessment of Educational Progress (NAEP; U.S. Department of Education, 1997) have remained essentially the same for all subjects assessed. The one positive trend in test scores, a significant improvement in the performance of African American and Hispanic students, mainly took place in the 1970s and has leveled off in the 1980s and 1990s; this trend even slightly reversed itself for the first time on the 1994 reading assessments. The best that can be said for the trends in student achievement is that despite public perceptions to the contrary, at least student achievement is not getting worse; on average, students today are doing as well as (but no better than) students in 1971, the year of the first NAEP assessment.

In every other field of endeavor, Americans expect progress. Imagine being satisfied that medicine or engineering were no worse today than in 1971. In fact, precisely because of dramatic advances in other technologies, the importance of a highly educated work-force is far greater today then ever before, and disparates in income between well-educated and poorly educated adults are growing rapidly. The sense of crisis and impatience expressed in *A Nation at Risk* (National Commission on Excellence in Education, 1983) and so many other commission reports is certainly justified. There may not in fact be a rising tide of mediocrity, but even a steady tide of mediocrity is bad enough, and cause for concerted action.

Even if average levels of student performance were adequate by international standards, there is a continuing crisis that still requires immediate and forceful action: the wide gap in achieve-ment between white and minority students, especially African American and Hispanic students. For example, on the 1994 NAEP, 29% of white fourth graders scored below the "basic" level in read-ing, but 69% of African American students and 64% of Hispanic students scored this poorly. It is not far-fetched to trace much of the enormous economic and social inequities that plague our society to those early differences in academic success. Yet the reforms of the past 15 years, often undertaken particularly in the name of low-income and minority students, have hardly dented this gap.

Why has the educational reform movement had so little impact on student achievement? The answer, we would argue, is that school reform has operated very far from the classroom and has had little impact on daily teaching and learning. The problem is that policymakers have focused overwhelmingly on issues over which they have more or less direct control: standards, assess-ments, accountability, governance, charters, choice, vouchers, pri-vatization, curricular frameworks, and so on. These are collectively referred to as "systemic reforms" (Smith & O'Day, 1991). Some sys-temic reforms, such as standards, are probably necessary, but all of them, at best, merely create conditions thought to be conducive to improvement in instruction or provide incentives for educators to do a good job. At worst, they amount to school bashing or teacher bashing, almost taking the position that if those lazy administrators and teachers would just work harder (under the threat of, say, dis-missal, reconstitution, or loss of schools to the private sector), then everything would be fine. Yet anyone who spends any time at all in schools knows that teachers and administrators are working very hard, doing the best they know how to do. As in any profession, there are bad apples and dead wood, but the numbers are small. Even removing the worst 10% of teachers and administrators, an enormously difficult process to undertake fairly, would not solve our problems. Although it is of course necessary to find better teachers and get rid of the ineffective ones, it is the hard working and dedicated 90% that we must reach if we expect to have a broad impact on student performance.

Recent research is finding that systemic reforms are not having much of an impact on classroom practice. State standards and assessments sometimes have an influence on what is taught, but they rarely have any effect at all on how well anything is taught (see Goertz, Floden, & O'Day, 1996; Newmann, King, & Rigdon, 1997). This should hardly be surprising to anyone. It is usually difficult to trace a logical path from regulations passed in Washington or Sacramento, Austin or Annapolis, to change in the everyday teaching behaviors of teachers in individual schools and classrooms. Yet it is impossible to imagine how student achievement will change unless there are profound changes in the instruction they receive.

Reform One School at a Time

Clearly, school reform must change the routine practices of teachers and administrators. Yet the challenge of doing school reform one school at a time is daunting. In the United States there are more than 2.6 million teachers in 85,000 public elementary and secondary schools in more than 15,000 school districts, not to mention 25,000 private schools. How can fundamental reforms be introduced on a large enough scale to make a difference with such an enormous number of teachers in such a diverse array of institutions? Proponents of systemic reform are not unaware of the need to change schools more directly, but they argue that there is no plausible strategy capable of transforming very large numbers of schools one at a time.

That situation is now changing. In recent years, there has developed an approach to school reform that is not entirely new, but that has begun to be applied with success on a massive scale. This approach emphasizes development of comprehensive, replicable approaches either to whole school reform or to innovations in a particular curriculum area, rigorous evaluation of the reform design comparing schools using the program to similar control schools, and construction of a network of trainers and participating schools capable of enabling large numbers of schools to adopt and successfully implement the designs. Whole-school reform designs, such as James Comer's School Development Project, Henry Levin's Accelerated Schools, and our own Success for All and Roots and Wings programs, are each used in as many as a thousand schools throughout the United States. New American Schools, a foundation funded primarily by large corporations, has supported the development of seven whole-school designs, collectively used in about 500 schools. Reading Recovery, a first-grade tutoring model, is in more than 6,000 schools, and other programs focused on particular subjects and grade levels are also very widely used.

The existence of these broadly replicated school change models, some of which have extensive and often-replicated evidence of effectiveness, profoundly changes the discussion about large-scale reform of America's schools. If it is in fact possible to *directly* improve teaching and learning in thousands of schools, to replicate excellence, then we need not rely exclusively on the roundabout path to reform embodied in the focus on standards, assessments, governance, and the like.

The advantages of reforming schools using replicable, well-developed, and well-evaluated models are many. First, they provide teachers with the tools to transform their daily instruction. Models vary in terms of their comprehensiveness and structure, but many provide innovative student materials, teacher's manuals, assessments, training and follow-up procedures, and other supports. Teachers need not reinvent the wheel. Most provide extensive, long-term assistance from trainers and from schools involved in the same program. For example, most conduct annual national and/or regional conferences, publish newsletters, and maintain electronic bulletin boards or other means to connect schools with each other and keep them up to date on the latest developments in the network. Many have definite standards of implementation, and work hard to see that these standards are met; some will exclude schools from the network if they do not meet a standard of implementation. The networks provide an external professional reference group for schools focused entirely on quality of teaching, which, being national rather than local, is not subject to the year-to-year political turmoil inherent to school districts. Schools experience changes in superintendents, principals, state policies, and funding levels every few years, but their reform network is always there for them. Participation in a reform network gives schools examples of good practice and a practicable goal to which they can jointly strive, as well as an identification with a high-status network of educators who speak a common language and support one another's efforts.

Because reform networks are preparing materials and strategies for many schools, they can do a far better job than schools working on their own. They can invest in talented developers, attractive materials, videos and software for use in training, and so on. Each school staff must adapt any reform design to meet its own needs, resources, and circumstances, but it is far easier for staffs to modify or adapt a complete and well-structured program than to make one up from scratch.

To the extent that reform designs are rigorously researched and well documented, they can give school staffs assurances that their efforts to undertake fundamental reforms are likely to pay off. No reform network can guarantee positive outcomes, as these depend on the quality of implementation (see, e.g., Herman & Stringfield, 1997; Schaffer, Nesselrodt, & Stringfield, 1997). However, to put in the extraordinary efforts necessary to implement fundamental classroom reforms across an entire school, the staff must have some well-founded confidence that if implemented with skill and care, the program will work. Similarly, building and district administrators, and the public at large, must have confidence that an investment in a reform process will lead to measurably enhanced outcomes.

The existence of well-evaluated programs able to work in large numbers of schools creates an unprecedented opportunity for policymakers to have a direct impact on classroom practice. When district, state, or federal policymakers allocate funds for generic "professional development," they have no idea (and little confidence) whether this will really make a difference. As a result, professional development funds are chronically scarce and are the first funds to be cut when finances are tight. In contrast, policymakers can have greater confidence that if they invest in a set of proven, replicable programs, there is likely to be a benefit. As an important example of this, the U.S. Congress recently approved an unprecedented allocation of funds to provide more than $50,000 per school for up to 3 years to help schools to adopt proven comprehensive designs (see Chapter 2). This bill would not have passed if legislators did not have confidence that schools could make a difference in student achievement if they implemented any of several whole-school models.

Of course, it is essential that school staffs have a voice in selecting school reform designs. For example, our Success for All and Roots and Wings programs require a vote of at least 80% of the professional staff, and go to great efforts to see that the staff are well informed about the model and are supportive of it. Similar buy-in strategies are used in many other programs. No matter how effective they are in their evaluations, no program should be imposed on an unwilling or uninformed staff. Some schools are simply not ready for major change, for one reason or another. However, when schools are ready, they need to have a means of quickly translating intentions into action and seeing results. Replicable programs provide a ready resource for school staffs impatient to improve student outcomes.

The Role of Research

Why is it that medicine, engineering, agriculture—in fact, most fields of endeavor—make steady progress over time in their basic technologies and effectiveness, whereas education moves from fad to fad with little apparent impact on student outcomes? Perhaps the most important reason is that in other fields, research is respected and used as a guide to practice, whereas in education this is hardly the case. Change in educational practice more resembles change in fashion; hemlines go up and down according to popular tastes, not evidence. We do give lip service to research in education. Yet practices from use of phonics in beginning reading to use of ability grouping in secondary schools go in and out of fashion, often in direct contradiction to well-established evidence, but more often in the absence of adequately rigorous and compelling research. Part of the problem is that the tiny national investment in educational research leads educators and policymakers to believe that educational research isn't doing very much, which leads to poor funding for research, in a continuing downward spiral.

Worse, many educators and academics do not believe in quantitative research at all, or believe that every teacher and every school must develop their own approach to school reform. Research and experience show just the opposite; well-developed, well-documented, and well-evaluated programs are far more likely to be implemented and maintained in schools than are programs that require teachers to create their own approaches (see, e.g., Bodilly, 1996).

When educators do insist on evidence, often the evidence is of doubtful quality. For example, many program developers obtain data from dozens of schools, and then only present data from those that showed the largest increase in test scores in a given year. Others show only gains from fall to spring in normal curve equivalents, long known to greatly overstate program effects (see Slavin & Madden, 1991). These and a variety of equally shoddy practices are sometimes difficult for educators to detect, especially when to do so would require tracking down original sources in hard-to-find publications. As a result, many educators who would otherwise value evidence become cynical, accepting all evidence as equally true (or false) and coming to believe that anything (or nothing) can be proved with statistics.

The most important purpose of this book is to give educators information on widely available programs, whose evaluations are tested against a consistent set of rigorous standards of evidence. Educational practice is unlikely to make lasting advances until educators demand to see the evidence, insist on control groups, and require full documentation of developers' claims.

A Policy Imperative

This book is written at a time of great danger and great opportunity for the reform of America's schools, particularly schools serving many students placed at risk. The danger is that after so many years of "reform," policymakers will decide that schools are simply intractable, and the impulse for reform will run out of steam. One concrete manifestation of this danger is represented by the disappointing results of *Prospects*, the national longitudinal study of Chapter 1 (Puma et al., 1997). This study found few positive effects of Chapter 1. The successor to Chapter 1, Title I, is somewhat different in structure, but unless Title I schools widely adopt programs known to make a difference, Title I is at risk. In 1997, there was a serious proposal in the House Committee on Education and the Workforce to zero out Title I. This did not pass, but without major changes in the programs it pays for, Title I will remain vulnerable. At $7.8 billion per year, Title I is the only substantial source of funding that high-poverty schools can use for reform. The reforms they choose must be likely to work.

On the other hand, there is also unprecedented opportunity for significant change. The 1994 reauthorization of Chapter 1 as Title I enabled schools in which at least 50% of students qualify for free lunch to implement Title I as a schoolwide project. They can use their Title I dollars flexibly to meet the needs of all children, not just those identified as low performing. Even in nonschoolwide Title I schools, there is a new emphasis on using Title I funds to enhance the quality of instruction, not just to provide remedial services or classroom aides.

Action in the U.S. Congress is creating additional possibilities. As noted earlier, recent legislation authorized competitive grants of at least $50,000 per year for schools to use to cover the start-up costs of adopting proven, comprehensive reform models. Two separate grants programs were formed, one ($120 million) for Title I schools and one ($25 million) for non–Title I schools. The possibilities of this legislation are revolutionary. For the first time, evidence of effectiveness could become an essential element in the school reform process. If continued over time, a funding program of this kind could provide an incentive for researchers and developers to create a wide variety of schoolwide reform models, specifically designed to be replicable and rigorously evaluated in comparison to control groups.

Scope of the Reviews

This book primarily consists of reviews of research on programs that could potentially be used by many elementary and secondary schools. A consistent set of criteria is applied to evidence from many sources on many programs. These are described in the following sections.

Effectiveness

Programs were considered to be effective if evaluations compared students who participated in the program to similar students in matched comparison or control schools and found the program students to perform significantly better on fair measures of academic performance. Such evaluations were required to demonstrate that experimental and control students were initially equivalent on measures of academic performance, socioeconomic status, and other measures, and were similar in other ways. "Fair measures" were ones assessing objectives pursued equally by experimental and control groups; for example, a curriculum-specific measure would be fair only if the control group were implementing the same curriculum.

Many studies of innovative programs used evaluations that compared gains made by program students on standardized tests, usually expressed in percentiles or normal curve equivalents (NCEs), to "expected" gains derived from national norming samples. This design, widely used in evaluations of Chapter 1/Title I programs, is prone to error and generally overstates program impacts (see Slavin & Madden, 1991). Programs evaluated using NCE gains or other alternatives to experimental-control comparisons are discussed as promising if their outcomes are particularly striking, but such data are not considered conclusive. We exclude after-the-fact comparisons of experimental and control groups chosen after outcomes are known.

Replicability

The best evidence that a program is replicable in other schools is that it has in fact been replicated elsewhere, especially if there is evidence that the program was evaluated and found to be effective in sites beyond its initial pilot locations. The existence of an active dissemination effort is also a strong indication of replicability. Programs are considered low in replicability if they have been used in a small number of schools and appear to depend on conditions (e.g., charismatic principals, magnet schools, extraordinary resources) unlikely to exist on a significant scale elsewhere.

Literature Search Procedures

The broadest possible search was carried out for programs that had been evaluated and/or applied to disadvantaged students. In addition to searches of the ERIC system and of education journals, we obtained reports on promising programs listed by the National

Diffusion Network (NDN). The NDN, which lost its funding in 1996, was part of the U.S. Department of Education that identified promising programs, disseminated information about them through a system of state facilitators, and provided "developer/disseminator" grants to help developers prepare their products for dissemination and then to carry out a dissemination plan. To be listed by NDN a program must have presented evidence of effectiveness to a Program Effectiveness Panel (PEP), or formerly to the Joint Dissemination Review Panel (JDRP). PEP or JDRP panel members reviewed the data for educationally significant effects. However, the evaluation requirements for PEP/JDRP have been low, and more than 500 programs of all kinds have been approved, mostly on the basis of NCE–gain designs (see National Diffusion Network, 1995).

Selection for Review

Ideally, programs emphasized in this book would be those that present rigorous evaluation evidence in comparison to control groups showing significant and lasting impacts on the achievement of students placed at risk, have active dissemination programs that have implemented the program in many schools serving at-risk students, and have evidence of effectiveness in dissemination sites, ideally from studies conducted by third parties. To require all of these conditions would limit this review to very few programs. To include a much broader range of programs, we had to compromise on one or more criteria. For example, we included programs with excellent data that show positive effects for students even if the program has not been widely replicated (as long as there is no obvious reason it could not be replicated). We have included programs that have shakier evidence of effectiveness if they are particularly well-known, widely replicated, and appropriate to the needs of Title I schools. In particular, we have listed widely known comprehensive schoolwide programs, even if the evidence supporting them is more anecdotal than conclusive. Thus, our listing of a program in this book is by no means a statement that we believe the program to be highly effective and replicable. Instead, it is an indication that among the hundreds of programs we have reviewed, these were the ones we felt to be most appropriate to be considered by elementary and secondary schools, especially Title I schools. We have tried to present the evidence that school and district staff would need to begin a process leading to an informed choice from among effective and promising programs capable of being replicated in their settings.

Effect Sizes

The outcomes of the evaluations summarized in this review are quantified as "effect sizes" (ES). These are computed as the difference between experimental and control group means divided by the control group's standard deviation (Glass, McGaw, & Smith, 1981). To give a sense of scale, an effect size of +1.0 would be equivalent to 100 points on the SAT scale, two stanines, 15 points of IQ, or about 21 NCEs. In general, an effect size of +0.25 or more would be considered educationally significant. When means and standard deviations are not known, they can usually be estimated from t tests, Fs, chi squares, or exact p values. If effect sizes cannot be computed, study outcomes are still included if they meet all other inclusion criteria. Because of differences between measures, experimental designs, and other factors, effect sizes should be interpreted with great caution. For example, effect sizes are almost always higher on experimenter-made tests closely aligned with program curricula than on more general standardized tests (see Rosenshine & Meister, 1994). However, effect sizes do provide a useful indication of programs' effects on student achievement that can be compared (with caution) across studies and programs.

Show Me the Evidence!

The evidence summarized in this book will be useful for educators and researchers looking for effective and replicable programs. However, we hope to have an additional and perhaps even more important impact: to get educators into the habit of asking for evidence of the kind we have emphasized here. We won't be satisfied if schools simply adopt the programs we've identified as effective; not until they begin to demand "Show me the evidence!" will education begin to build the scientific basis that is critical to forward progress in any field.

2

Schoolwide Programs[1]

◆

In school reform, sometimes, the whole can be greater than the
sum of its parts.

Although replicable programs for various subjects and grade
levels have long existed, only in the past decade has there
appeared in many schools a new kind of design for whole-school
reform. Whole-school designs are intended to affect just about
everything schools do, from curriculum and instruction to professional development to school organization. Some whole-school
designs provide schools with specific curriculum materials or curriculum approaches, whereas others provide more general guidelines for curriculum and involve teachers in creating or adapting
their own approaches.

Whole-school reform networks have learned how to work
intensively with schools on a very large scale. Some approaches,
such as Henry Levin's Accelerated Schools, James Comer's School
Development Project, and our own Success for All and Roots and
Wings designs, are each serving 600 to 900 schools. Whole-school
designs must be adapted to local circumstances, resources, and
needs, but they are designed to be replicated across a broad range
of circumstances. This large-scale capacity means that any school
willing to meet the networks' financing, buy-in, and implementation quality standards is likely to be able to join one of them and to
receive substantial assistance through the change process.

There are important advantages of whole-school designs. A
commitment by all school staff to a common vision allows schools

to take on issues of school organization, climate, policies, and other features that would not generally be addressed in a school accumulating innovations in specific curriculum areas. A whole-school approach increases the likelihood that all aspects of the reform process will be well coordinated with each other. Working with a single reform organization is easier and less likely to lead to confusion or contradictory policies. Traditional approaches to educational innovation have been described as being like hanging ornaments on a Christmas tree, with many disconnected programs coexisting in the same building. Whole-school reform replaces the entire tree.

The greatest potential impact of the new whole-school designs is on two categories of schools. One is Title I schools in which at least 50% of students qualify for free or reduced-price lunches. Under the 1994 reauthorization of Chapter 1 as Title I, these schools can use their Title I resources to serve all children in the school, not just low achievers, and there is a strong push in Title I to focus such schools on proven whole-school designs. Already, Title I schoolwide projects are by far the largest users of whole-school designs, especially the School Development Project and Success for All/ Roots and Wings, and it is among such schools that the most rapid growth in program adoptions is taking place.

The second group of schools most likely to adopt whole-school designs in the future are those that take advantage of the 1997 Obey-Porter amendment that sets aside funds for Title I as well as non–Title I schools to adopt proven, comprehensive designs. Schools will be able to apply for grants of at least $50,000 for up to 3 years to cover the start-up costs (e.g., materials and training) inherent to the adoption of comprehensive designs, such as those described in this chapter.

With both of these groups of schools, as well as many others, the stakes are high. As noted earlier, the *Prospects* evaluation of Chapter 1 (Puma et al., 1997) found few positive effects of participation in the program, and this finding has threatened continued funding of this crucial resource for high-poverty schools. The primary difference between Chapter 1 and its successor, Title I, is that Title I facilitates schoolwide status. Therefore, making schoolwide projects effective is essential for building confidence in the overall Title I program. The comprehensive program adoption legislation also provides wonderful opportunities as well as great dangers. If educators can demonstrate markedly better achievement as a result of the adoption of proven practices, support for research as well as for professional development linked to research are likely to expand. If this opportunity is perceived to fail, the opposite outcome may occur.

This chapter reviews research on whole-school programs designed to affect all core aspects of school functioning: instruction, curriculum, classroom management, assessment, professional development, and governance. These programs are designed, evaluated, and disseminated by a variety of organizations: universities, nonprofit R&D organizations, and for-profit organizations. Programs were included if they had national capacity to work with large numbers of schools and have been extensively used with Title I schoolwide projects and other schools. Evidence of effectiveness was not required for a program to be reviewed; programs listed in this chapter should by no means all be considered "proven," but they are certainly promising, ambitious, comprehensive, and widely available. They were selected for review primarily on the basis that among all programs that we might have considered, these are ones that Title I schoolwide projects, other Title I schools, and non–Title I schools might legitimately consider as systemic alternatives to what they are doing now, with some confidence that should they choose them there are sources of assistance available to help them with the adoption process.

Schoolwide Reform Programs

Success for All

The schoolwide reform program that has been most extensively evaluated in schools serving many students placed at risk is Success for All, a comprehensive reform program for elementary schools serving many children placed at risk (Slavin, Madden, Dolan, & Wasik, 1996). Success for All provides schools with innovative curricula and instructional methods in reading, writing, and language arts from kindergarten to Grade 6, with extensive professional development. The curriculum emphasizes a balance between phonics and meaning in beginning reading and extensive use of cooperative learning throughout the grades. Recently, programs in mathematics, social studies, and science have been added to Success for All, making up a program called Roots and Wings (Slavin, Madden, & Wasik, 1996), described in a later section.

One-to-one tutoring, usually from certified teachers, is provided to children who are having difficulties in learning to read, with an emphasis on first graders. Family support services provided in each school build positive home-school relations and solve problems such as truancy, behavior problems, or needs for eyeglasses or health services. A program facilitator works with all teachers on continuing professional development and coaching, manages an assessment program to keep track of student progress, and ensures close coordination among all program components.

In schools with Spanish bilingual programs, Success for All uses Spanish materials with instructional strategies similar to those used in the English program, but uses a curriculum sequence and materials appropriate to Spanish language and Latino culture (called *Lee Conmigo* for Grade 1 and *Alas Para Leer* for Grades 2-6). In schools with many limited English proficient students that teach in English, there is a close coordination between ESL and classroom reading programs to infuse effective ESL strategies into the reading approach.

Longitudinal research on the Success for All program has taken place in 23 schools in nine districts throughout the United States. In each case Success for All schools were matched with similar comparison schools. Students were pretested to establish comparability and then individually posttested each year on scales from the Woodcock Reading Mastery Test and the Durrell Oral Reading Test. Results show consistent, substantial positive effects of the program, averaging an effect size of about +0.50 at each grade level. For the most at-risk students, those in the lowest 25% of their grades, effect sizes have averaged more than a full standard deviation (ES = +1.00 or more). In grade-equivalent terms, differences between Success for All and control students have averaged 3 months in the first grade, increasing to more than a full grade equivalent by fifth grade (Slavin, Madden, Dolan, Wasik, Ross, et al., 1996). Follow-up studies have found that this difference maintains into sixth and seventh grades, after students have left the program schools. A study of 49 Success for All schools in Houston found that the full program is significantly more effective than partial implementations, especially in the highest-poverty schools (Nunnery et al., 1996). Studies of special education find that Success for All substantially reduces special education placements (Smith, Ross, & Casey, 1994) and has a strong positive impact on the achievement of children already in special education (Ross, Smith, Casey, & Slavin, 1995).

For language minority students, the effects of Success for All have been particularly positive (Slavin & Madden, 1995). Bilingual schools using *Lee Conmigo* in Philadelphia found substantial differences between Success for All and control schools on scales from the Spanish Woodcock, with an effect size at the end of second grade of +1.81 (almost a full grade equivalent different). A study in two California bilingual schools (Dianda & Flaherty, 1995) also found very positive effects of Success for All/*Lee Conmigo*. At the end of first grade, Success for All students exceeded control students by an effect size of +1.03, or about 5 months. Dianda and Flaherty (1995) also reported an effect size of +1.02 for Spanish-dominant LEP students in a sheltered English adaptation of Success for All in a third California school. Incidentally, a 5-year study of the ESL adaptation of Success for All to limited English proficient Cambodian students in Philadelphia also found extremely positive outcomes, averaging an effect size of +1.44 and a grade equivalent difference of almost 3 years by the end of fifth grade (Slavin & Madden, 1995).

As of fall 1997, Success for All is in use in more than 750 schools in 36 states, nearly all Title I schools. A training staff in Baltimore, with regional training programs in many parts of the U.S. and Canada, disseminates the program nationally; program adaptations are also used in Mexico, Australia, Israel, and England.

Roots and Wings

Roots and Wings (Slavin, Madden, Dolan, & Wasik, 1994; Slavin, Madden, & Wasik, 1996) is a comprehensive reform design for elementary schools that adds to Success for All innovative programs in mathematics, social studies, and science. Funded by New American Schools, Roots and Wings has recently begun to be disseminated nationally.

Roots and Wings schools typically begin by implementing all components of Success for All, described above. In the second year of implementation they typically begin to incorporate the additional major components. *MathWings* is the name of the mathematics program used in Grades 1-5. It is a constructivist approach to mathematics based on NCTM standards but designed to be practical and effective in schools serving many students placed at risk. MathWings makes extensive use of cooperative learning, games, discovery, creative problem solving, manipulatives, and calculators.

WorldLab is an integrated approach to social studies and science that engages students in simulations and group investigations. Students take on roles as various people in history, in different parts of the world, or in various occupations. For example, they work as engineers to design and test efficient vehicles, they form a state legislature to enact environmental legislation, they repeat Benjamin Franklin's experiments, and they solve problems of agriculture in Africa. In each activity students work in cooperative groups, do extensive writing, and use reading, mathematics, and fine arts skills learned in other parts of the program.

A study of Roots and Wings (Slavin, Madden, & Wasik, 1996) was carried out in four Title I schools in rural southern Maryland. The assessment tracked growth over time on the Maryland School Performance Assessment Program (MSPAP), compared to growth in the state as a whole. The MSPAP is a performance measure on which students are asked to solve complex problems, set up experiments, write in various genres, and read extended text.

In both third- and fifth-grade assessments in all subjects tested (reading, language, writing, math, science, and social studies), Roots and Wings students showed substantial growth. On every measure, the percentage of students scoring at the "satisfactory" or "excellent" levels gained substantially more than the average for all Maryland schools. Evaluations of MathWings in San Antonio and in Miami and Palm Beach County, Florida, have also found strong positive effects (Madden, Slavin, & Simons, 1997).

As of fall 1997, approximately 70 schools have added MathWings and/or WorldLab to their implementations of Success for All, making themselves into Roots and Wings schools.

Edison Project

The Edison Project is a comprehensive, schoolwide reform model launched by media entrepreneur Chris Whittle. Edison, a for-profit organization, contracts with local school districts to run all aspects of selected schools. They select their own principals and staff, use their own curricula and professional development, and adhere to their own rules, although they accept any students who wish to attend. The program mandates a longer school day (7-8 hours) and school year (205 days). It usually provides extensive computers and software, including computers for students to take home.

Most Edison curriculum and instruction is borrowed from other programs. In elementary reading, writing, and language arts, Edison schools use Success for All, including the early childhood, tutoring, and family support components. It uses the University of Chicago School Mathematics Project for math in all grades, and the Scholastic Company's Science Place program. To these, it adds a comprehensive system of performance assessments, learning contracts, and professional development.

The Edison Project is in early stages of implementation but has begun formal evaluations of its pilot sites. The first year evaluation focused primarily on reading performance in Grades K-2. Schools in Wichita, Kansas, and Mt. Clemens, Michigan, were assessed on the same individually administered reading measures used in Success for All evaluations (see Edison Project, 1996). The Wichita evaluation showed the largest impacts. Compared to matched children in control groups, Edison kindergartners averaged .26 grade equivalents higher across four measures (ES = +.68); the differences for first graders averaged .23 grade equivalents (ES = +.37). Second grade differences were nonsignificant.

At the Mt. Clemens, Michigan Edison school, kindergarten students gained almost 2 months more than controls, on average (ES = +.48), and first graders also gained almost 2 months more than controls (ES = +.36).

The experimental-control differences in kindergarten and first-grade reading performance found in Wichita and Mt. Clemens are similar to those found in other Success for All evaluations (Slavin, Madden, Dolan, & Wasik, 1996; Slavin, Madden, Dolan, Wasik, Ross, et al., 1996), so it is as yet unclear how much the rest of the Edison design adds to this effect. However, Edison is early in its development and evaluation, and it seems likely that the other program components will have an additional impact as the project reaches full implementation in each school.

As of fall 1997, Edison will be in approximately 15 elementary schools, 8 middle schools, and one high school nationwide.

Direct Instruction/DISTAR

Direct Instruction (DI), or DISTAR (Bereiter & Engelmann, 1966) is an early elementary school program originally designed to extend the Direct Instruction early childhood curriculum into the elementary grades as part of a federal program called Follow Through, which funded the development and evaluation programs to continue the positive effects of early childhood programs. The primary goal of both the early childhood program and DI was to provide low–SES children with opportunities to succeed academically by utilizing a scripted program that stresses structured direct instruction.

Teachers involved in Direct Instruction have specific instructions on how to teach each of the units presented to the students, as well as what units to teach them. Students initially begin with DI in either kindergarten or first grade. Progress in DI is usually monitored by evaluating academic performance of students in the program, using both criterion-referenced and norm-referenced measures.

The most comprehensive evaluation of Direct Instruction compared the results of nine Follow Through programs that also had early-childhood education programs. Each program was compared to control groups that were not implementing DI (Abt Associates, 1977). The total number of subjects was 9,255 for the DI (experimental group) and 6,485 for the non–DI students.

All of the children were from similar socioeconomic backgrounds. The study evaluated the effects of the programs on academic achievement, cognitive achievement, and self-esteem, as measured by performance on norm-referenced tests such as MAT, Ravens Progressive Matrices (1956), Coopersmith Self-Esteem Inventory, and the Intellectual Achievement Responsibility Scale.

Direct Instruction and Behavior Analysis were the only models that showed substantial effects in all three areas both when compared to non–Follow Through programs and when compared to other programs. Other programs evaluated showed either effects of zero, or negative effects when all three of the skills (basic, cognitive, or affective) were measured. The Direct Instruction group did better than all of the other groups on the MAT language (ES = +.84) and mathematics computation (ES = +.57). Direct Instruction students also scored somewhat higher in reading comprehension (ES = +.07) and mathematics problem solving (ES = +.17) and were also higher in self-esteem.

In addition to the Follow Through evaluations, there have been many smaller-scale evaluations that have also shown strong positive effects of Direct Instruction in reading (Adams & Engelmann, 1996). Most of these have involved special education, where the program's effects have been particularly large.

Becker and Gersten (1982) studied the lasting effects of Direct Instruction on students in fifth and sixth grades. This study followed up students who had been in DISTAR in Grades 1-3 in five sites, in comparison to students in matched control groups. Overall results show that DI students outperformed non–DI students on the overall WRAT (ES = +.53), and on all of the subtests of the MAT.

Meyer (1984) investigated the long-term effects of DISTAR on children who had had 3 and 4 years of the program and compared their achievements to those of matched control groups. The study involved three cohorts of students from a New York City elementary school. Students in the Direct Instruction Follow-Through school in New York City were compared to matched control students as high school seniors on graduation rate, ninth-grade reading score, ninth-grade math score, student's application to college, student's acceptance to college, student's special education placement, and student's school attendance for the previous year. More than 63% of the Direct Instruction students graduated from high school, as opposed to 38% of the control group. An average of 21% of the Direct Instruction students were retained, compared to 33% of the control students. The Direct Instruction students had a lower drop-out rate (28%) than the control group (46%). More of the Direct Instruction (34%) group students applied to college than the control group (22%), and more of the Direct Instruction group students were accepted for admission to college over the three cohorts (34%) than were the control group students (17%). Overall, ninth graders in the Direct Instruction cohort outperformed students in the control group in reading (ES = +.41) and in math (ES = +.29).

Direct Instruction is most often used as a basal reading approach or as the curriculum for special education or remedial programs. However, it can also be used as a whole-school reform model. A Baltimore experiment currently under way, the Baltimore Curriculum Project, combines DI, Core Knowledge (see below), and other elements to create a schoolwide design affecting all elementary subjects and grade levels.

The current version of Direct Instruction is commercially published and used throughout the U.S.

Core Knowledge

Core Knowledge is an approach to curriculum and instruction based on the work of E. D. Hirsch (1987). The main emphasis of the approach is on teaching a common core of concepts, knowledge, and skills that define an educated individual. The curriculum itself is defined in a series of books titled *What Your (First, Second, etc.) Grader Needs to Know* (Hirsch, 1991a, 1991b, 1992a, 1992b, 1993b, 1993c). The hallmark of the curriculum is specificity. From very early on, children are taught about Egypt, Greece, Rome, and ancient African kingdoms; about photosynthesis, space, and Mayan calendars; about Shakespeare, haiku, and the Harlem Renaissance. In addition to the curriculum sequence, the Core Knowledge Foundation provides teachers with general guidelines and examples of how to teach the various topics (Core Knowledge Foundation, 1995).

Core Knowledge is more a set of curriculum standards than it is a school reform model, and therefore it is difficult to evaluate in comparison to traditional conceptions of curriculum. The question of what should be taught, especially in such subjects as social studies and science, is often a question of values, which are not empirically testable. However, the program does make claims in terms of test outcomes.

A study by Stringfield and McHugh (1997), currently in its second year, compares six Baltimore Core Knowledge schools to six matched control schools. Outcomes are very inconsistent. On the district's Comprehensive Tests of Basic Skills, Core Knowledge first graders scored slightly better than controls in reading comprehension (ES = +.09), with larger positive differences in math concepts (ES = +.18). Third graders also scored slightly higher than controls in reading (ES = +.08), but no different in math. On the Maryland School Performance Assessment Program, a state-of-the-art performance measure that would seem on its face to be more appropriate to Core Knowledge, differences were equally inconclusive. Core Knowledge third graders gained slightly more than controls on math, social studies, writing, and language use scales; were essentially identical in reading; and scored worse than controls in science. Among fifth graders, Core Knowledge students gained slightly more (or declined slightly less) than controls on MSPAP reading, math, social studies, and science scales, and there were no differences in writing. The only important experimental-control differences were on language usage.

Preliminary second-year data show similar patterns: slight and inconsistent advantages for the Core Knowledge schools (S. Stringfield, personal communication, May 20, 1997). Anecdotal information from Core Knowledge schools in San Antonio, Texas (Schubnell, 1996) and Albemarle County, Virginia (Marshall, 1996) have found higher-than-expected reading performance.

Core Knowledge makes few claims to improvements in basic skills, and the evidence to date is not encouraging in these areas. As a schoolwide change model Core Knowledge might best be seen as part of a larger intervention, with other programs providing basic reading and math skills. For example, a program currently being implemented in six Baltimore elementary schools combines Core Knowledge with Direct Instruction reading, and Core Knowledge is part of the more comprehensive Modern Red Schoolhouse design, described elsewhere in this paper.

Core Knowledge is currently used in more than 350 schools in 40 states throughout the United States.

Accelerated Schools

Accelerated Schools (Hopfenberg & Levin, 1993; Levin, 1987) is an approach to school reform built around three central principles. One is *unity of purpose,* a common vision of what the school should become, agreed to and worked toward by all school staff, parents, students, and community. A second is *empowerment coupled with responsibility,* which means that staff, parents, and students find their own way to transform themselves, with freedom to experiment but also a responsibility to carry out their decisions. *Building on strengths* means identifying the strengths of students, of staff, and of the school as an organization and then using these as a basis for reform. One of the key ideas behind Accelerated Schools is that rather than remediating students' deficits, students who are placed at risk of school failure must be accelerated, given the kind of high-expectations curriculum typical of programs for gifted and talented students.

The school implements these principles by establishing a set of *cadres* that include a steering committee and work groups focused on particular areas of reform. The program has no specific instructional approaches and provides no curriculum material; instead, school staff are encouraged to search for methods that help them realize their vision. However, there is an emphasis both on reducing all uses of remedial activities and on adopting constructivist, engaging teaching strategies (such as project-based learning).

The evaluation evidence on Accelerated Schools is quite limited and largely anecdotal. The program's developers state that the program takes 5 years to fully implement and that it is unfair to evaluate program outcomes until that much time has passed. No evaluation evidence has yet been reported from schools in the program this long. However, data from a few individual schools earlier in their implementations have been reported. McCarthy and Still (1993) reported on one Texas school with a large Latino majority that showed gains over time in its fifth-grade standardized test scores (other grades were not mentioned). A similar comparison school showed losses over the same period. Knight and Stallings (1995) reported mixed results, some favoring an Accelerated School and some a control school.

More than 900 schools in 39 states are currently involved in the Accelerated Schools network, and there are four regional training sites for the program in addition to the original training site at Stanford.

School Development Program

The School Development Program (SDP; Comer, 1980, 1988; Comer, Haynes, Joyner, & Ben-Avic, 1996) is a comprehensive approach to school reform in elementary and middle schools. The program's focus is on building a sense of common purpose among school staff, parents, and community, and engaging school staff and others in a planning process intended to change school practices to improve student outcomes.

Each SDP school creates three teams that take particular responsibility for moving the reform agenda forward. A School Planning and Management Team, made up of representatives of teachers, parents, and administration, develops and monitors implementation of a comprehensive school improvement plan. A

Mental Health Team, principally composed of school staff concerned with mental health such as school psychologists, social workers, counselors, and selected teachers, plans programs focusing on prevention, building positive child development, positive interpersonal relations, and so on.

The third major component of the SDP is a Parent Program, designed to build a sense of community among school staff, parents, and students. The Parent Program incorporates existing parent participation activities (such as the PTA) and implements further activities to draw parents into the school, increase opportunities for parents to provide volunteer services, and design ways for helping the school respect and celebrate the ethnic backgrounds of its students.

The three teams in SDP schools work together to create comprehensive plans for school reform. Whereas the main focus is on mental health and parent involvement, schools are also encouraged to examine their instructional programs and to look for ways to serve children's academic needs more effectively.

The SDP was originally designed especially to meet the needs of African American children and families, but large numbers of Latino and white students also attend SDP schools.

Evaluations of the effects of SDP have taken place in a number of locations. The first was a longitudinal evaluation of the first two SDP schools in New Haven, Connecticut, which showed marked improvements in student performance on standardized tests during a 14-year period (Comer, 1988). The Special Strategies study, which followed first graders in two SDP schools, also showed positive effects of the SDP model (Stringfield, Millsap, & Herman, 1997). Other evaluations comparing SDP to matched control schools have found mixed, inconsistent effects, with substantial site-to-site variation. Outcomes emphasized by the program, such as self-concept and school climate, have been more consistently associated with the program than have achievement gains (Becker & Hedges, 1992; Haynes, 1991, 1994).

The SDP is currently involved with more than 565 schools, mostly elementary and middle schools in 22 states. It has regional training programs in several states.

Consistency Management and
Cooperative Discipline (CMCD)

Consistency Management and Cooperative Discipline (CMCD) (Freiberg, Prokosch, & Treister, 1990) is a schoolwide reform program designed to improve discipline in inner-city schools at all grade levels. CMCD emphasizes shared responsibility for classroom discipline between students and teachers, turning classrooms into communities of ownership, where the teachers and students together make the rules for classroom management. The idea is that if students have a hand in creating and enforcing the rules, then acting up to defy the teacher would not work anymore, *because (students) would also be breaking their own laws* (Freiberg et al., 1990).

CMCD provides a framework of regulations, which schools adapt to fit their needs. The main components or themes of CMCD that exist at every school are prevention, caring, cooperation, organization, and community. At the initial implementation stages of CMCD, the teachers engage in a series of interviews and assessment sessions, whose goals are to evaluate the school's strengths and weaknesses and adapt the program to fit their school.

CMCD has primarily been evaluated in inner-city schools in Houston, with many African American and Latino students. The main evaluation of CMCD followed five CMCD and five matched control schools in Houston during a period of 5 years (Freiberg, Stein, & Huang, 1995). This evaluation found significant positive effects on standardized achievement tests, especially for students who remained in the program for 6 years (Freiberg & Huang, 1994; Freiberg et al., 1995).

The most recent study of CMCD (Freiberg, 1996) compared the performances of students in schools implementing a mathematics program with those in schools implementing a combination of CMCD and the mathematics program. All of the schools involved in this study were majority Latino. The students in the combined program outperformed students involved in the mathematics only program, with an effect size of +.33.

CMCD currently exists in more than 25 schools in three Texas districts, plus schools in Chicago and Norfolk. It is establishing a national dissemination capacity.

Coalition of Essential Schools

The Coalition of Essential Schools is a network of schools (almost all secondary) engaged in a process of reform guided by the theories of Theodore Sizer (1984, 1992, 1996). The schools build their approach around nine "common principles":

1. Schools should have an intellectual focus.
2. Schools' goals should be simple.
3. Schools should have universal goals that apply to all students.
4. Teaching and learning should be personalized.
5. The governing metaphor should be student as worker, teacher as coach.
6. Diplomas should be awarded upon demonstration of mastery.
7. The tone of the school should stress unanxious high expectations.
8. Principals and teachers should view themselves as generalists first and specialists second.
9. Teacher load should be 80 or fewer students, and per-pupil cost should not exceed traditional school costs by more than 10%.

By design, schools participating in the Coalition are expected to create their own paths to reform. The Coalition headquarters, at Brown University, provides very little training to schools or materials to guide reform; instead, it provides forums in which school leaders can come together to share ideas, promotes collaboration among schools, and gives schools feedback on their efforts. In practice, Coalition schools tend to emphasize block scheduling (double periods), project-based learning, and *exhibitions* (demonstrations of competence in a given area), but other elements (such as 80-to-1 student to teacher ratios) are rarely seen.

Research on the outcomes of the Coalition schools has focused on descriptions of what was implemented rather than on student outcomes, and therefore these do not meet the effectiveness criteria applied in this book.

It is important to note that Sizer does not value or claim impacts on standardized tests, and there are no studies using measures of achievement that Sizer or like-minded reformers would find acceptable. However, it is worthwhile for educators to be aware of the limited evidence that does exist.

The *Special Strategies* study (Stringfield, Millsap, et al., 1997) evaluated five schools nominated as exemplary by the Coalition. During a 3-year period, these schools showed no gains in reading comprehension, and generally lost ground in mathematics, compared to national norms. Absenteeism increased in two of three schools. A Chicago study of 11 schools found dropping test scores, graduation rates, and attendance (Sikorski, Wallace, Stariha, & Rankin, 1993). As these studies lacked control groups and used only standardized measures with limited relationships to what was actually being taught in the schools, they should not be seen as conclusive, but what is important is the absence of countervailing evidence on any measures of student achievement in other research. For example, there is no reason that measures of creative writing or math problem solving could not have been used to evaluate Coalition schools on measures more closely aligned with the program, yet such studies do not exist. Implementation studies in Coalition schools find enormous difficulties in putting Coalition principles into practice; for example, a longitudinal study by Muncey and McQuillan (1996) of eight schools, as well as the *Special Strategies* and Chicago studies, found few indicators that most Coalition principles were ever implemented in more than a few classrooms.

As of 1996, the Coalition reported involvement with more than 1,000 schools nationally but claimed only 238 as "member schools" actively working on reform (Sizer, 1996).

Paideia

The Paideia program, based on the work of Mortimer Adler (1982), emphasizes engaging all students in intellectual inquiry, with a particular focus on great books and great thinkers. It uses small-group "Socratic" seminars, coaching by teachers, peer tutoring, project-based learning, and other means of engaging students as active learners. As with the Coalition and Accelerated schools, Paideia principles are used as a general guide to reform, not a specific strategy.

There is very little research evaluating Paideia. One Chicago study (Wallace, 1993) did find higher attendance and achievement among Paideia students in magnet schools than among other high school students, but there was no indication that these groups were initially equivalent. A writing assessment showed substantial growth in writing for secondary students, but very high attrition in the control group made experimental-control comparisons invalid. The *Special Strategies* study (Stringfield, Millsap, et al., 1997) followed two Paideia elementary schools during a 3-year period. Students progressing from Grades 3 to 5 achieved at about the same level as comparison schools on measures of reading and math, whereas they declined in attendance rates.

New American Schools Designs

The development of comprehensive, schoolwide designs for school reform has been greatly advanced by the New American Schools Development Corporation (NASDC), now called New American Schools (NAS). Founded in 1991, NAS is a foundation primarily funded by large corporations to support the development and dissemination of ambitious school designs for the 21st century. Initially, 11 design teams were funded to develop school designs. Four were discontinued for various reasons. The remaining seven are now engaged in national dissemination.

With the exception of our own Roots and Wings program, described earlier, the NAS designs are at too early a stage of implementation and evaluation to have produced conclusive outcome data. Most have anecdotal data noting outstanding gains in one or two schools (among many that might be using the program). However, although the achievement data supporting them are limited so far, these designs have several features that make them attractive alternatives for Title I schoolwide projects and other schools seeking fundamental reform. First, these designs are very comprehensive. To one degree or another, all address curriculum, instruction, school operation, assessments, and parent/community involvement. Second, all are built for replication. All of the designs provide trainers, well-specified professional development strategies, and networks of implementing schools that help mentor new schools into the network.

In addition to Roots and Wings, the New American Schools designs are as follows (see Stringfield, Ross, & Smith, 1996, for more details).

ATLAS Communities

The ATLAS Communities (Comer, Gardner, Sizer, & Whitla, 1996) is a design based on a collaboration among four school reform organizations, those led by James Comer, Howard Gardner, Theodore Sizer, and Jane Whitla. ATLAS incorporates elements of Comer's (1988) School Development Project, described earlier, but also adds elements from the other reform networks and also has several unique features unique to it. One of these is a focus on working with pathways, feeder systems of elementary, middle, and high schools whose staff work with each other to create coordinated and continuous experiences for students. The emphasis of the design is on helping school staffs create classroom environments in which students are active participants in their own learning, putting into practice a model (following Sizer's [1992] Coalition of Essential Schools) of student as worker, teacher as coach. Project-based learning is extensively used. Assessment in ATLAS schools emphasizes portfolios, performance examinations, and exhibitions.

Preliminary data from implementing schools show some gains. In Prince George's County, Maryland, reading test scores increased by up to 30% in one ATLAS elementary school, and a middle school reported increases on test scores in math, language arts, science, and social studies on the Maryland School Performance Assessment Program.

Audrey Cohen

The Audrey Cohen College System of Education (Cohen & Jordan, 1996) is based on the teaching methods used at the Audrey Cohen College in New York City. This design attempts to have all learning relate to a purpose that contributes to the community or world at large. Each semester's work is built around a purpose, such as using science and technology to shape a just and productive society, or helping people through the arts. Curriculum materials appropriate to the semester's purpose are identified or adapted for schools' use. Academic activities build toward "constructive action" projects in which children apply knowledge to contribute to real community needs.

Anecdotal reports of early outcomes have identified individual schools implementing Audrey Cohen design in San Diego, Phoenix, and Miami that have reported above-average gains on standardized achievement tests.

Co-NECT

Co-NECT (Goldberg & Richards, 1996) is a design created at a Cambridge (MA) consulting firm, Bolt, Beranek, and Newman. The design focuses on complex interdisciplinary projects that extensively incorporate technology and connect students with ongoing scientific investigations, information resources, and other students beyond their own school. Cross-disciplinary teaching teams work with clusters of students. Performance-based assessments are extensively used.

On a battery of performance items, one of the original pilot schools for Co-NECT, a middle school in Worcester, Massachusetts, showed significant gains from 1994 to 1995 in reading scores. Other schools also showed gains in selected areas.

Expeditionary Learning

Expeditionary Learning/Outward Bound (Campbell et al., 1996) is a design built around learning expeditions, explorations within and beyond school walls. The program is affiliated with Outward Bound and incorporates many of its principles of active learning, challenge, and teamwork. It makes extensive use of project-based learning, cooperative learning, and performance assessments.

Expeditionary Learning schools in Boston, Dubuque, and New York City have shown significant increases over time on standardized test scores.

Modern Red Schoolhouse

The Modern Red Schoolhouse (Kilgore, Doyle, & Linkowsky, 1996) was begun as a project of the Hudson Institute, a conservative think tank in Indianapolis. The program emphasizes strong core academic subjects, and in the elementary and middle grades is based on the E. D. Hirsch (1993a) core curriculum. It makes extensive use of technology in instruction and assessment and has established benchmarks for academic performance that all students must achieve to be advanced into the next unit or grade.

Several elementary schools involved in the Modern Red Schoolhouse design have shown improvement on standardized tests in the early grades. In particular, a school in the Bronx showed substantial gains on a state essential skills test in reading and math.

National Alliance

The National Alliance for Restructuring Education (Rothman, 1996) is a partnership of states, school districts, and national organizations affiliated with the New Standards Project. The National Alliance is different from all other NAS designs in that its emphasis is more on systemic reform than on specific school-by-school restructuring. In particular, the National Alliance works to help states and districts establish standards, performance assessments, and accountability methods, and then helps schools design their own approaches to meet those standards. Districts are also urged to give schools greater autonomy and control over resources to find their own ways to meet high standards. In the state of Kentucky, a key National Alliance partner, schools engaged with the National Alliance were much more likely than other Kentucky schools to earn awards for improving their students' performance.

Summary of Outcomes

As noted earlier, an ideal program for this book would be one that had been rigorously evaluated many times in elementary or secondary schools serving students placed at risk and had been extensively replicated in such schools. However, few programs would meet all of these criteria. Table 2.1 summarizes the degree to which each of the programs reviewed met these inclusion criteria. The table is only a summary; see Fashola and Slavin (1997) for more detail on the characteristics, evaluation evidence, and replicability of each program.

TABLE 2.1 Categorization of Schoolwide Programs Reviewed

Program Name	Grades Served	Meets Evaluation Criteria for Achievement?	Widely Replicated?
Schoolwide Reform Programs			
Success for All	K-6	Yes	Yes
Roots and Wings	K-6	Yes	Yes
Edison Project	K-12	Yes (for primary program)	No
Direct Instruction/ DISTAR	K-6	Yes	Yes
Core Knowledge	K-6	Partially	Yes
Accelerated Schools	K-8	Partially	Yes
School Development Program (SDP)	K-8	Partially	Yes
Consistency Management and Cooperative Discipline (CMCD)	K-12	Yes	No
Coalition of Essential Schools	6-12	No	Yes
Paideia	K-12	No	Yes
New American Schools Designs			
ATLAS Communities	K-12	Partially	Yes
Audrey Cohen	K-12	Partially	Yes
Co-NECT	K-12	Partially	Yes
Expeditionary Learning/ Outward Bound	K-12	Partially	Yes
Modern Red Schoolhouse	K-12	Partially	Yes
National Alliance	K-12	Partially	Yes

Assembling Components

Title I schoolwide projects and other schools seeking whole-school reform can greatly expand their range of alternatives by assembling their own set of components into a comprehensive model. A key advantage of comprehensive models is that their developers have thought through an overall school plan and know how to coordinate each of the elements of that plan with each other, how to phase them in over time, and so on. However, a school staff can certainly create its own plan and work out for itself how the elements will connect with each other.

There is a very broad range of programs in particular subject areas from which schools can select. Obviously, there are many commercial textbooks and other programs that provide professional development as well as materials. The National Diffusion Network (NDN), terminated in 1996, listed more than 500 replicable programs with some evidence of effectiveness, most of which were innovations in particular subjects and grade levels. Despite the demise of NDN, many of these programs still exist; for a list, see National Diffusion Network, 1995.

In building a schoolwide model from components that are themselves proven (but subject-specific) models, there are three key types of interventions schools should look for, as follows.

1. *Curriculum and Instruction.* The most important set of interventions are those that affect what happens between children and teachers every day. Schools should review instructional programs in each major area of the curriculum, focusing on approaches that have evidence of effectiveness in comparison to matched control groups. (A list of elementary and secondary programs with good evidence of effectiveness appears in the following chapters.) These tend to provide extensive professional development, far beyond that ordinarily provided by commercial textbook programs. Because of this, it is usually important to phase in curricular and instructional innovations over a period of time, ensuring high-quality implementation of each element before the next is introduced.

Improving the quality of classroom instruction is the best and most cost-effective means of improving overall student achievement and preventing at-risk students from falling behind. In addition to extensive professional development, effective models tend to provide for a great deal of classroom follow-up from expert and/or peer coaches. They usually provide extensive curriculum-based assessment to enable teachers to continually adjust their pace and level of instruction and to identify individual children in need of extra assistance. Teachers implementing innovative curricula should have regular opportunities to meet to discuss what they are doing, to visit each others' classes, and to share materials and ideas.

2. *Programs for At-Risk Students.* Even with the best of instruction, some number of students in any school will always experience academic difficulties. An overall school plan must provide services for these children. In general, the best approaches to helping struggling students catch up with their peers involve one-to-one assistance targeted to the unique needs of the student. Most effective are tutoring programs involving certified teachers, such as those used in Reading Recovery (Pinnell, Lyons, DeFord, Bryk, & Seltzer, 1994) and in Success for All/Roots and Wings (Slavin, Madden, Dolan, & Wasik, 1996; Slavin, Madden, Dolan, Wasik, Ross, et al., 1996). However, tutoring approaches using paraprofessionals (Wasik & Slavin, 1993), volunteers (Wasik, 1997), and cross-age peer tutors (Cohen, Kulik, & Kulik, 1982) can also be effective. In each case, tutoring and other supportive services are likely to work best if they are closely linked to classroom instruction, using the same materials and objectives but adapting teaching methods to students' needs.

3. *Family Support.* Any comprehensive schoolwide reform approach should include elements designed both to engage parents in support of their children's success in school and to solve nonacademic problems that could interfere with children's school performance. Such programs are a part of almost all of the schoolwide approaches discussed earlier, and there are many parent-focused programs that have their own dissemination programs, such as Parents as Teachers (Pfannenstiel, Lambson, & Yarnell, 1991) and Teachers Involve Parents in Schoolwork, or TIPS (Epstein, Salinas, & Jackson, 1995). In addition, schools should consider approaches to integrate health, mental health, and social services with their educational programs. One national model for this is Schools of the 21st Century (Zigler, Finn-Stevenson, & Linkins, 1992).

Conclusion

The results of *Prospects,* the most recent national evaluation of Chapter 1 (Puma et al., 1997), like others before it, give little to validate those who would support traditional practices in high-poverty Title I schools. Providing small-group remedial services to children who have already fallen behind has never been found to be effective for at-risk children. The 1994 reauthorization of Chapter 1 as Title I gives schools with at least 50% of their students in poverty an opportunity to use Title I funds as a fuel for comprehensive schoolwide reform. To take advantage of these opportunities, however, schools need to have access to a broad range of proven and replicable options, to enable them to make rational, considered choices among programs that work rather than trying to reinvent the wheel. In addition, the 1997 congressional allocation for adoption of proven comprehensive designs gives all schools a similar opportunity.

This chapter describes schoolwide reform models that are nationally available and summarizes the evidence of effectiveness for each. It also describes a strategy for assembling effective subject-specific instructional innovations, programs for struggling students, and family support programs into well-coordinated schoolwide plans. It is apparent from the discussions of the currently available schoolwide reform models that much more research is necessary to truly have available a substantial "shelf" of proven models. Yet what we do know now is that schools need not start from scratch in designing effective schoolwide plans. A wide array of promising programs are readily available, backed up by national networks of trainers, fellow users, materials, assessments, and other resources. For most Title I schoolwide projects and other schools ready for major reform, it is probably a better use of time and resources to affiliate with one of these networks and then work out how to implement their models with integrity, intelligence, and sensitivity to local needs and circumstances than to try to develop a completely new approach.

Schoolwide projects are not a magic pill to cure the ills of America's schools; it matters a great deal which particular model schools choose and how effectively they implement it. Yet it is clear that schools can turn their Title I and other dollars into markedly better achievement for their children and that models able to facilitate this process are replicable and are widely available. Not every school needs to adopt one of these models, but they do provide a standard against which home-grown models should be assessed.

Note

1. This chapter is adapted from Fashola and Slavin (in press b).

3

Classroom
Instructional Programs[1]

◆

M ost of the replicable programs currently available to schools
are classroom instructional programs, typically focusing on a
single subject and grade span. For example, among the more than
500 programs listed by the National Diffusion Network (1995), the
great majority are classroom innovations. This chapter presents
research on classroom instructional programs that are widely available and well evaluated.

Because there are so many more classroom instructional programs than schoolwide programs, the selection criteria for listing
in this chapter are more stringent than for those in the preceding
chapter. Programs are listed here only if they have credible evidence of effectiveness and are broadly available. The National
Diffusion Network (1995) book should be consulted for a broader
listing of classroom innovations with dissemination capacity and
some evidence of effectiveness, at least in some schools.

Cooperative Learning Methods

Cooperative learning refers to a broad range of instructional
methods in which students work together to learn academic content. Research comparing cooperative learning and traditional
methods has found positive effects on the achievement of elementary and secondary students, especially when two key conditions

are fulfilled. First, groups must be working toward a common goal, such as the opportunity to earn recognition or rewards based on group performance. Second, the success of the groups must depend on the individual learning of all group members, not on a single group product (see Slavin, 1995).

Cooperative learning methods are widely used throughout the United States and other countries with all kinds of schools and children, and the research on these methods has equally involved a broad diversity of schools and students.

Cooperative Integrated Reading and Composition (CIRC) and Bilingual Cooperative Integrated Reading and Composition (BCIRC)

Cooperative Integrated Reading and Composition, or CIRC (Stevens, Madden, Slavin, & Farnish, 1987), used in Grades 2-8, involves a series of activities derived from research on reading comprehension and writing strategies. Students work in four-member heterogeneous learning teams. After the teacher introduces a story from a basal text or trade book, students work in their teams on a prescribed series of activities relating to the story. These include partner reading, where students take turns reading to each other in pairs; "treasure hunt" activities, in which students work together to identify characters, settings, problems, and problem solutions in narratives; and summarization activities. Students write "meaningful sentences" to show the meaning of new vocabulary words, and write compositions that relate to their reading. The program includes a curriculum for teaching main idea, figurative language, and other comprehension skills, and includes a home reading and book report component. The writing/language arts component of CIRC uses a cooperative writing process approach in which students work together to plan, draft, revise, edit, and publish compositions in a variety of genres. Students master language mechanics skills in their teams, and these are then added to editing checklists to ensure their application in students' own writing. Teams earn recognition based on the performance of their members on quizzes, compositions, book reports, and other products (see Madden et al., 1996).

BCIRC (Calderón, Hertz-Lazarowitz, & Slavin, in press; Calderón, Tinajero, & Hertz-Lazarowitz, 1992) adds to the CIRC structure several adaptations to make it appropriate to bilingual settings. It is built around Spanish reading materials in the younger grades and then uses transitional reading materials as students begin to transition from Spanish to English. The age of transition depends on district policies; materials to accompany Spanish basals and novels have been developed though the sixth grade, but most such materials are used in transitional bilingual education programs only through the third or fourth grades. In addition, effective ESL strategies designed to engage students in negotiating meaning in two languages and increase authentic oral communication are built into the training program.

The original CIRC program has been evaluated in three studies in elementary schools (Stevens et al., 1987; Stevens & Slavin, 1995) and one study in two middle schools (Stevens & Durkin, 1992). In each case, CIRC students made significantly greater gains than control students on standardized tests of reading achievement. Two studies in Israel, one in Hebrew and one in Arabic, also found positive effects of CIRC compared to traditional methods (Hertz-Lazarowitz, Lerner, Schaedel, Walk, & Sarid, 1996; Schaedel et al., 1996).

A 4-year study of BCIRC was conducted in 24 Grade 2-4 bilingual classes in El Paso, Texas (Calderón et al., in press). Experimental and control classes were carefully matched. Students transitioned from mostly-Spanish instruction in second grade to mostly-English instruction in the fourth grade. At the end of second grade, BCIRC students scored significantly better than control on the Spanish TAAS (Texas Assessment of Academic Skills) in both reading (ES = +.43) and writing (ES = +.47). In third grade, students were tested on the English Norm-Referenced Assessment Program for Texas (NAPT), and again BCIRC students outperformed controls in reading (ES = +.59) and language (ES = +.29). Finally, fourth graders in BCIRC scored higher than controls in NAPT reading (ES = +.19), but not language. However, these differences were depressed by the transfer of students out of the bilingual classes into English-only classes, which happened with four times as many BCIRC as control students. Students who were moved out of the bilingual classes early tended to be the highest achievers, so deleting them from the sample reduced the apparent experimental-control differences.

CIRC is used in several hundred schools nationally, and BCIRC is used in more than a hundred. In addition to their separate uses, both are part of Success for All in the upper elementary grades (see

Chapter 2). Training programs for CIRC and BCIRC exist at Johns Hopkins University in Baltimore and El Paso, and additional trainers in both models are located in many parts of the United States.

Complex Instruction/Finding Out/Descubrimiento

Complex Instruction is the name given to a set of cooperative learning approaches developed and researched by Elizabeth Cohen (1994a) and her associates at Stanford University. From its inception, the program has focused on Spanish bilingual classes. It was first built around a discovery-oriented science and mathematics program called Finding Out/Descubrimiento, developed by DeAvila and Duncan (1980). Finding Out/Descubrimiento provides students with a series of activity cards in English and Spanish that direct them to do experiments, take measurements, solve problems, and so on. Students work in small heterogeneous groups to do experiments and answer questions intended to evoke high-level thinking. As it relates to bilingual education, a major focus of the program is to get students to use complex, sophisticated language to express, debate, and defend their ideas, thereby building language fluency first in their home language and then in English. Whenever possible, each group contains monolingual Spanish, monolingual English, and bilingual children, who freely translate ideas for each other. Complex Instruction adds to Finding Out/Descubrimiento a group structure, in which students take on specified roles (e.g., facilitator; checker, reporter) and learn group process skills, such as active listening, maintaining a positive group atmosphere, and ensuring equal participation. The program also emphasizes building positive expectations for all students; for example, by giving low-status children opportunities to be the group expert and constantly reinforcing the idea that all children have different abilities, each of which is worthy of respect (Cohen, 1994a).

The evaluations of Complex Instruction/Finding Out/Descubrimiento have not generally met the standards established in this book. Most have reported positive correlations between the frequency of students' talking and working together and gains in student achievement (Cohen, 1984; Cohen & Intili, 1981; Cohen, Lotan, & Leechor, 1989; Stevenson, 1982). This could be taken as an indication that better implementers of the program get better results, but it does not indicate that the children are performing better than they would have without the program. Similarly, reports of NCE gains in the program classes (see Cohen, 1994b) are inadequate indicators of program impacts. Still, the accumulation of imperfect but supportive evidence and the clear focus on improving the higher-order thinking of students in bilingual programs makes this program appealing.

The Complex Instruction program at Stanford provides materials and professional development to support program adoption in elementary and middle schools, and it is used in many schools, particularly in California.

Student Teams–Achievement Divisions and Teams-Games-Tournaments

Two related cooperative learning programs developed at Johns Hopkins University are among the most thoroughly evaluated of all cooperative methods and have been extensively disseminated. These are Students Teams–Achievement Divisions (STAD) and Teams-Games-Tournament (TGT) (Slavin, 1994, 1995). In STAD, students work in four-member, heterogeneous learning teams. First the teacher provides the lesson content through direct instruction. Then students work in their teams to help each other master the content, using study guides, worksheets, or other material as a basis for discussion, tutoring, and assessment among students. Following this, students take brief quizzes, on which they cannot help each other. Teams can earn recognition or privileges based on the improvement made by each team member over his or her own past record. TGT is the same as STAD except that students play academic games with members of the other teams to add points to an overall team score. Both programs emphasize the use of group goals (in this case, recognition) in which teams can only achieve success if each team member can perform well on an independent assessment. This motivates team members to do a good job of teaching and assessing each other.

Both STAD and TGT have been extensively evaluated in comparison to control groups in a wide variety of subjects, mostly in schools serving many African American and/or Latino students. Across 26 such studies of at least 4 weeks duration, there was a median effect size of +.32 for STAD; in 7 studies of TGT, the median effect size was +.38 (Slavin, 1995).

STAD and TGT are used in thousands of classrooms nationwide. A training program at Johns Hopkins University and certified trainers throughout the United States provide professional development in these methods.

Jigsaw

Jigsaw (Aronson, Blaney, Stephan, Sikes, & Snapp, 1978) is a cooperative learning technique in which students work in small groups to study text, usually social studies or science. In this method, each group member is assigned to become an "expert" on some aspect of a unit of study. After reading about their area of expertise, the experts from different groups meet to discuss their topic and then return to their groups and take turns teaching their topics to their groupmates. In a variation of Jigsaw called Jigsaw II (Slavin, 1994), students are given topics in a common reading, such as a text chapter, biography, or short book. After they have read the material, discussed it with their counterparts in other groups, and shared their topics with their own group, they take a quiz on all topics, as in STAD.

The first brief Jigsaw evaluation (Lucker, Rosenfield, Sikes, & Aronson, 1976) found positive effects of the program for "minority students" (Latino and African American students analyzed together), but not for Anglos. A study in bilingual classes (Gonzales, 1981) and one in majority-Latino schools (Tomblin & Davis, 1985) found no achievement benefits. Outcomes for Jigsaw II have been more positive (Mattingly & Van Sickle, 1991; Ziegler, 1981).

Jigsaw is widely used nationwide. Training in numerous Jigsaw variations is provided by Spencer Kagan and his colleagues (Kagan, 1995), among others.

Learning Together

David and Roger Johnson's (1994) Learning Together models of cooperative learning are among the most widely used of all cooperative learning models. In these methods, students work in small groups on common assignments, typically creating a single group product. All group members are evaluated based on this product. In some applications of this method, groups may earn recognition or grades based on either overall group performance or on the sum of individual performances.

Many evaluations of Learning Together models have been very brief, but among those of at least 4 weeks' duration, evidence supports the achievement effects of forms of the Learning Together model that incorporate group goals and individual accountability (i.e., group success depends on the sum of individual performances).

The Johnsons' methods are widely used throughout the world. Trainers in these methods are located at the University of Minnesota and in many other parts of the United States.

Curriculum-Specific Programs: Reading, Writing, and Language Arts

There are many well-evaluated and replicable programs designed for use in specific grades and subjects. In reading, positive effects have been found in the Success for All and CIRC programs, described earlier, and in three additional programs described in this section. Positive reading effects have also been found for tutoring programs, described in a later section. In writing and language arts, effective methods generally include some form of process writing, in which students work together to plan, draft, revise, edit, and publish compositions. A general review of process writing models (Hillocks, 1984) found consistently positive effects on quality of students' writing. CIRC and BCIRC, described earlier, use process writing methods. Other approaches to writing that have been successfully researched and/or disseminated with students placed at risk are described below.

Exemplary Center for Reading Instruction

The goal of the Exemplary Center for Reading Instruction (ECRI; Reid, 1989) is to improve elementary students' reading ability. This program emphasizes such reading-related skills as word recognition, study skills, spelling, penmanship, proofing, and writing skills, leading to improvement in decoding, comprehension, and vocabulary.

ECRI teachers expect all students to excel. The lessons for ECRI are scripted and incorporate multisensory and sequential methods and strategies of teaching. In a typical lesson, teachers introduce new concepts in lessons using at least seven methods of instruction, teaching at least one comprehension skill, one study skill, and a grammar/creative writing skill. Initially, students are prompted for answers by teachers. As the students begin to master the information presented, fewer and fewer prompts are provided until students can perform independently.

In one evaluation (Reid, 1989), researchers investigated the effects of ECRI on students in Grades 2-7 in Morgan County, Tennessee, and compared them to students in a control group who were using a commercial reading program. Both schools were tested using Stanford Achievement Test reading comprehension and vocabulary subtests. ECRI students outperformed those in the control group, with effect sizes ranging from +.48 to +.90 in reading comprehension, and from +.31 to +1.40 in vocabulary. Evaluations of ECRI in Oceanside, California; Killeen, Texas; and Calexico, California (Reid, 1989), showed NCE gains that ranged from +6.4 to +25.7. ECRI is used in hundreds of schools nationwide.

Reciprocal Teaching

Reciprocal Teaching (Palincsar & Brown, 1984) is a reading program designed to improve the reading comprehension of children in elementary and middle schools that emphasizes cognitive strategies of scaffolding through dialogue.

The main two components of Reciprocal Teaching are comprehension fostering, which includes the four strategies of question generation, summarization, prediction, and clarification; and dialogue, which includes prepared conversations and questions that guide the comprehension process and product. The program uses a scaffolding process, in which teachers are initially more responsible for producing questions, guiding the dialogue, and showing the students how to comprehend text. Eventually, the students become more responsible for the products, creating questions for each other and guiding the dialogue with less teacher input.

A typical Reciprocal Teaching session begins with students reading an initial paragraph of expository material, with the teacher modeling how to comprehend the paragraph. The students then practice the strategies on the next section of the text, and the teacher supports each student's participation through specific feedback, additional modeling, coaching, hints, and explanation. The strategies include commenting and elaborating on summaries of paragraphs, suggesting additional questions, providing feedback on their peers' predictions, and requesting clarification of material not understood.

A meta-analysis of the achievement effects of Reciprocal Teaching was carried out by Rosenshine and Meister (1994). Sixteen studies representing different levels of implementation (high, medium, and low) and different methods of teaching were synthesized. High-implementation studies included dialogue, questions, and assessment of student learning strategies; medium-level studies included dialogue but did not include assessments; and low-level studies had neither dialogue nor assessment information.

The meta-analysis investigated how Reciprocal Teaching students performed on standardized and experimenter-made tests as compared to their control-group peers. The overall effect size for performance on standardized tests was +.32; but only in two cases did the Reciprocal Teaching students do significantly better on standardized tests than their control group counterparts. Effect sizes were much higher on the experimenter-made tests (ES = +.88). In several cases, effect sizes were lower in studies in which implementations were rated as low in quality, but there were few differences between the outcomes of high- and medium-quality implementations.

Profile Approach to Writing (PAW)

The Profile Approach to Writing (PAW; Hartfiel, Hughey, Wormuth, & Jacobs, 1985; Hughey & Hartfiel, 1979; Hughey, Wormuth, Hartfiel, & Jacobs, 1985; Jacobs, Zinkgraf, Wormuth, Hartfiel, & Hughey, 1981; PAW, 1995) is a program that provides professional development in creative writing to students in Grades 3-12. The program emphasizes a process of drafting and revision of compositions, and makes use of a writing profile to assess and guide student writing performance. The profile is a holistic/analytic scale that assesses content, organization, vocabulary use, language use, and mechanics in students' compositions.

Several evaluations of the Profile Approach to Writing have been carried out by the program developers (PAW, 1995). One of these compared students in a predominantly (55%) Latino middle school in Texas to a control group. Students in the experimental and control group were pre- and posttested on the project's own Composition Profile, the 100-point holistic/analytic scale used in the instructional program. Experimental and control students were similar in scores at pretest. Students in the PAW school gained significantly more than those in the control group (ES = +.69) in a 1-year-long comparison. Other less-well-controlled evaluations on district-administered tests also found positive effects of PAW in middle and high schools.

A methodological limitation of the main experimental-control comparison is the fact that it used the project's own evaluation instrument, which teachers and students had been using all year. However, holistic/analytic writing comparisons of this kind are common in many writing performance measures and are widely accepted by writing curriculum experts.

The replicability of PAW has been amply demonstrated. The program is in use in more than 1,000 schools and has certified trainers in seven states.

Multi-Cultural Reading and Thinking (McRAT)

Multi-Cultural Reading and Thinking (McRAT) is a writing program that trains teachers to improve students' academic achievement by adding multicultural themes to all areas of the curriculum in Grades 3-8. The program, developed by the Arkansas Department of Education (Arkansas Department of Education, 1992; Quellmalz, 1987; Quellmalz & Hoskyn, 1988), is intended to make students better readers and writers by adding multicultural and problem-solving components to all areas of the curriculum. McRAT does not exist as a stand-alone program, but works with the existing school curriculum. It strives to teach children to think critically about what they read in class, so that they can apply these critical processes to their writing and to real-life situations in which people of different backgrounds have to learn to work and live together. Specific skills that the children are taught include analysis, comparison, inference/interpretation, and evaluation, and these skills are used in all areas of the curriculum.

In the study that evaluated the effects of McRAT on achievement, students represented a range of socioeconomic status backgrounds, achievement levels, and ethnic backgrounds. This evaluation (Arkansas Department of Education, 1992) studied the effects of McRAT on achievement scores in the specific cognitive areas that the students were taught in the program. McRAT students were compared to matched control students.

The students in the treatment group were 32% minority, 15% gifted and talented, and 25% Title I students. In the control group, the students were 30% minority, 15% gifted and talented, and 10% Title I students. Students in both the experimental and control groups were using the same curriculum, the only difference being that students in the experimental group had McRAT-trained teachers. Students in this sample included 234 fourth-, fifth-, and sixth-grade McRAT students, and 106 fourth-, fifth-, and sixth-grade non–McRAT students. Students in both groups were assessed using an assessment measure created by the experimenters in September and again in May. The McRAT students outperformed the control students in the areas of analysis (ES = +.41), inference (ES = +.57), comparison (ES = +.65), and evaluation (ES = +.45). McRAT joined the National Diffusion Network in 1993, is currently used in 44 schools in Arkansas, and is also being disseminated nationally.

Curriculum-Specific Programs: Mathematics

Five mathematics programs met the inclusion standards applied in this review.

Comprehensive School Mathematics Program (CSMP)

The Comprehensive School Mathematics Program (CSMP, 1995), is a math program for Grades K-6 that emphasizes problem solving rather than drill-and-practice lessons. CSMP strives to teach children the mathematical thinking skills and concepts that they need to use when approached with new math problems. The contents of the CSMP curriculum range from basic skills such as addition and subtraction to more abstract skills such as probability, statistics, and classification using higher-order thinking skills, understanding of concepts, and algorithmic thinking. The program incorporates the use of calculators and computers.

CSMP uses different types of "languages" for performing different types of mathematical functions. The language of strings, for example, is used to gather data; the language of arrows places the different components of the mathematical problem into sets; and the language of a minicomputer allows the children to compute different problems using an abacus. Students also use manipulatives, such as tiles and blocks, to solve their problems.

Two research designs were used to evaluate CSMP (CSMP, 1995). The first design controlled for teacher effects: Teachers taught the regular curriculum during the first year and the CSMP curriculum during the second year. In the second design, CSMP classes were matched with a control group studying the regular curriculum. In both designs, students were given a problem-solving test called Mathematics Applied to Novel Situations test (MANS), which was created by the experimenters. The CSMP students outscored the control students in the second, third, and sixth grades, with effect sizes of +1.26 +.22, and +.30, respectively. In the fourth and fifth grades, the non–CSMP students outperformed the CSMP students, with effect sizes of -.16 and -.32, respectively.

CSMP was developed, evaluated, and initially disseminated by CEMREL, a former education laboratory in St. Louis. It is now disseminated by another educational laboratory (MCREL, in Aurora, CO) and has been used in districts throughout the United States.

Cognitively Guided Instruction (CGI)

Cognitively Guided Instruction (CGI; Carey, Fennema, Carpenter, & Franke, 1993; Carpenter, Fennema, Peterson, Chiang, & Loef, 1989) is a mathematics program designed to develop student problem solving in the early elementary grades. CGI was created to teach the teachers of first-grade students about problem-solving processes that their students use when solving simple arithmetic and complex mathematics problems and to train the teachers to create curricula consistent with new understandings of how children learn. Following extensive training, CGI teachers create units and themes to last the entire school year.

In an evaluation of CGI (Carpenter et al., 1989), 40 teachers were randomly assigned to either a control or a treatment group. CGI as well as control teachers had volunteered to participate in a summer inservice program that would last 4 weeks, and also to be observed in their classroom during instruction in mathematics during the following year. Teachers in both of the groups were involved in problem-solving workshops, but one was a CGI workshop and the other was a generic problem-solving workshop.

Teachers in the CGI workshop, for instance, learned that they should closely relate problem solving to basic skills competency and that problem solving should be the main focus of the mathematics lessons. They also learned that students should use prior knowledge when solving problems and be able to link what they already know to new problems that they may be solving. Teachers in the CGI workshop learned about teaching children conceptual problem solving, and the teachers were familiarized with curricular materials available for instruction. Finally, GCI teachers were asked to write a mathematics curriculum, based on what they had learned at the CGI workshops, that would span the academic year.

Teachers in the control groups also participated in problem-solving exercises for a similar amount of time. The teachers learned about the general concept of problem solving but did not discuss how to understand how children solve problems or how to write a curriculum that would help children to solve problems based on this information.

All students were given the Iowa Test of Basic Skills (ITBS) Level 6 as a pretest in September, and the computation subtest of the ITBS Level 7 was used as the written posttest of computation in April-May. Interviews were also conducted with the students.

Student achievement results showed that CGI students outscored their control group counterparts in computations (specifically in number facts) and in problem solving that involved complex addition/subtraction. Interviews also found that treatment students had better attitudes toward math and felt more confident that they could perform complex mathematics.

A second study of CGI evaluated the effectiveness of the program among low-income minority students (Villaseñor & Kepner, 1993). Twelve experimental and 12 control teachers were randomly assigned to CGI and control classes in Milwaukee. Minority populations ranged from 57% to 99%, primarily Latino or African American. A 14-item arithmetic word-problem test focusing on higher-level cognitive processes (Carpenter et al., 1989), developed by the creators of CGI, was administered as a pretest in early October, and again as a posttest in late February and early March. Controlling for small pretest differences, the experimental students outscored their control-group counterparts.

CGI is currently being implemented in several states, and

training programs for the model have been established in Wisconsin, North Carolina, and Ohio.

Project SEED

Project SEED (Hollins, Smiler, & Spencer, 1994; Johntz, 1966, 1975; Phillips & Ebrahimi, 1993; Project SEED, 1995) is an enrichment mathematics program designed to teach elementary school students, particularly low-income and minority students, to develop confidence in their ability to be successful in all academic work, giving them the grounding to help them to face challenging academic situations. Students participating in Project SEED are helped to improve their mathematics achievement skills and to continue to take classes in abstract and advanced mathematics.

Project SEED hires and trains mathematicians, scientists, and engineers to teach students in the targeted population. Project SEED mathematics specialists then go into the classroom and introduce abstract mathematical concepts using a discovery method based on Socratic questioning, always making students active participants in the lessons. The Project SEED curriculum does not take the place of the regular mathematics curriculum but is a supplement to it. When the Project SEED mathematics specialists teach the students, the regular classroom teachers remain in the classroom and observe and participate in what is being taught. Students involved in the program are expected to learn using dialogue, choral responses, discussion, and debates. In addition to teaching the students, the Project SEED mathematics specialists conduct workshops with the regular classroom teachers. Part of ongoing staff development includes Project SEED mathematics specialists' observing and critiquing each other in the classroom at work and attending internal workshops.

A study that evaluated the effects of one semester of Project SEED in Detroit (Webster & Chadbourn, 1992) compared the California Achievement Test (CAT) scores of 244 fourth-grade students in SEED classrooms to those of 244 fourth-grade students in SEED schools, but not in SEED classrooms (non–SEED), and to those of 244 fourth-grade students neither in SEED schools nor in SEED classrooms (comparison group) during the 1991-1992 academic year. Students in all three groups were matched based on gender, ethnicity, free or reduced lunch status, and third-grade CAT scores.

The SEED students outscored comparison group students in total math scores (ES = +.37), math computation (ES = +.38), and math concepts (ES = +.32). The non–SEED students in SEED schools also outscored the comparison students in all three areas, with effect sizes of +.17, +.23, and +.13, respectively. When the SEED and non–SEED schools were compared, students in the SEED group also outperformed students in the non–SEED groups on math total (ES = +.19), math computation (ES = +.16) and math concepts (ES = +.19).

The effect of one semester of SEED was also evaluated in Dallas in a Project SEED longitudinal evaluation study (Webster & Chadbourn, 1992). The Dallas evaluation involved 11 elementary learning centers (South Dallas Learning Centers and West Dallas Learning Centers). Students in the South Dallas Learning Centers were 80% African American, and students in the West Dallas Learning Centers were mostly Latino. There was a total of 10,890 Project SEED and matched comparison students. The treatment students were those who had been involved in Project SEED for at least one semester between 1982 and 1991. The test scores of the control and experimental groups were equivalent at the beginning of the experiment. As with the Detroit study, SEED students significantly outscored the non–SEED students on ITBS mathematics scales.

The cumulative effects of Project SEED on students after one, two, and three semesters of involvement were also investigated (Webster & Chadbourn, 1992). A total of 3,092 students in five different settings were matched with control students on the basis of grade level, total mathematics achievement score, gender, ethnicity, and socioeconomic status, as determined by free lunch program participation. Beginning in the fourth grade, students in the treatment group received either one, two, or three semesters of Project SEED. Students were matched with students in other schools who did not receive SEED instruction but may have received other types of intervention. Students were pretested on the ITBS, and after 1991, the Norm Referenced Achievement Test for Texas (NAPT). In every case except 1 out of 30 comparisons, the Project SEED students significantly outperformed the students in the control groups on the posttests for both the NAPT and the ITBS, and the more semesters that a student had been involved in Project SEED (up to the maximum of three semesters), the greater the cumulative effect of Project SEED.

A follow-up study (Webster & Russell, 1992) sought to evaluate the retention of mathematics skills after students had left Project SEED. This study included a total of 1,215 matched students from the previous study. Students who had been involved in the project for only one semester were followed for 5 years after their involvement, and students who had received three semesters of Project SEED in Grades 4-6 were followed through the 1991-1992 school year. Overall, all Project SEED students, regardless of how long they had been in the program, still outscored the non–SEED students on the ITBS/NAPT up to 2 years after their Project SEED participation ended. More specifically, students who had been involved in Project SEED for one semester retained their mathematics skills for at least 2 years after they had left the program, and students who had been involved in the program for three semesters still retained their skills between 2 and 5 years after they had left the program.

In the final Dallas longitudinal follow-up study of Project SEED (Webster, 1995), results showed that students who had been involved in Project SEED were more likely to enroll in advanced mathematics classes in the 9th, 10th, and 11th grades than were students who had not been involved in Project SEED.

Project SEED currently exists in Texas, Michigan, Indiana, Pennsylvania, and California (see Project SEED, 1995).

Skills Reinforcement Project (SRP)

The Skills Reinforcement Project (SRP, Mills, 1992; SRP, 1984, 1995; Skills Reinforcement Project, 1992) was developed by the Johns Hopkins University Center for Talented Youth (CTY). CTY began as a program for gifted or "highly able" students, but it later added SRP, which is specifically designed for use with minority or low-socioeconomic students who are likely to be underrepresented in advanced mathematics. The program was written to prepare fifth-through eighth-grade students to succeed in advanced level mathematics, with hopes that they would eventually become involved in mathematics and science careers.

Staff in schools that adopt SRP attend training sessions before the implementation and during the year. SRP schools have a coordinator, who oversees the general management of the program at the school and also oversees teacher training, curriculum development, and program evaluation. In addition to this, SRP schools involve a site director who acts as a facilitator for the program.

Students involved in the SRP program are volunteers. They attend Saturday school during the school year, and then they participate in a 2-week summer residential program. Students are initially assessed, and then teaching is based on the results of this testing. The SRP program provides a balance of individualized instruction and cooperative learning. The content of the SRP curriculum ranges from arithmetic concepts and skills to more advanced areas of study such as algebra, geometry, and statistics.

Research on SRP has been done at two sites in California, at schools with populations that are 40% African American, 40% Latino, and 20% other, with a majority of the minority students qualifying for free lunches. The research design for all of the evaluations consisted of pre-post experimental/control comparisons. Student participants in both the control and treatment groups were volunteered by parents and had to score between the 80th and 95th percentiles on the California Achievement Test. Students who met the criteria were randomly assigned to the SRP and control conditions, where the experimental students received substantial additional mathematics instruction, and the control group students received no extra mathematics instruction. The students were also equivalent on the basis of gender, ethnicity, income level, and mean pretest scores.

In addition to the CAT, the Sequential Tests of Educational Progress II (STEP) were used as pre- and posttests. The School and College Ability Test (SCAT) was used to assess mathematical reasoning ability.

The first evaluation was done in Pasadena, California (Lynch & Mills, 1990). In this study, 32 SRP and 32 control sixth graders were administered the CAT and the STEP while they were in the sixth grade, and again 9 months later in the fall of seventh grade. Adjusting for pretest differences, SRP students outperformed their control group counterparts (ES = +.41).

A replication study was also done in Pasadena (*Skills Reinforcement Project*, 1992). This study involved 38 students: 19 in the control group and 19 in the experimental group. In this study also, SRP students outscored the control group on both the SCAT (ES = +.72) and on the CAT/STEP tests (ES = +.73).

The third evaluation was done in Los Angeles (Mills, Stork, &

Krug, 1992). This study involved 54 students: 28 SRP students and 26 students in the control group. Once again, SRP students outscored the students in the control group on the SCAT (ES = +.55) and on the CAT/STEP (ES = +1.35).

It is important to note that the evaluation of SRP does not compare one instructional method to another but instead compares additional mathematics instruction to no extra instruction.

SRP is currently being used in three California school districts.

Maneuvers With Mathematics

Maneuvers With Mathematics (MWM) was founded at the University of Illinois at Chicago (Long, 1993; *Maneuvers With Mathematics*, 1995; Page, 1989). This program was designed to teach students in Grades 5-8 advanced mathematics problem solving. The goal of MWM is to motivate students to use mathematics in a creative manner, while still learning basic arithmetic skills. MWM trainers attend training sessions in summer institutes.

An emphasis of MWM is on training both the teachers and students to use calculators to solve both simple arithmetic and complex geometry and advanced mathematics problems. Students are shown how math is used every day, for example in cooking, traveling, building houses, and using money. They use specific books created by MWM, which stress problem solving, rechecking answers, and using mathematics in real-life situations. Teacher guides provide alternative ways of presenting topics and concepts to the students.

The main evaluation of this program was done in 1991. This evaluation involved 617 MWM students matched with 223 control students (*Maneuvers With Mathematics*, 1991). The students in both groups exceeded the state norms in mobility and in the number of low-income, limited-English-proficient (LEP) students. At the beginning of the year, students in both groups were administered pretests created by the Second International Mathematics Study (SIMS) and the National Assessment of Educational Progress (NAEP). The same tests were also used as posttests at the end of the school year. Students were not allowed to use calculators on these tests.

Adjusting for pretest differences, the MWM students outpeformed the students in the control group (ES = +.47). At each individual grade level, MWM students made better gains than the students in the control groups (ES = +.12, +.54, +.59, and +.86 in the fifth, sixth, seventh, and eighth grades, respectively).

MWM is validated by the National Diffusion Network and currently exists in all 50 states nationwide.

Curriculum-Specific Programs: Early Childhood

One way to increase the probability that students will succeed in school is to provide them with high-quality experiences before they enter school. This section briefly reviews research on Head Start, the source of prekindergarten programs for most disadvantaged students, and on two specific approaches to early childhood education. In addition, preschool and kindergarten curricula are part of the Success for All/Lee Conmigo and Roots and Wings programs, described earlier.

Head Start

The largest federal investment in early childhood education is Project Head Start (Zigler & Muenchow, 1992; Zigler & Valentine, 1973). Head Start began as one of President Johnson's War on Poverty programs in 1965. The goal of Head Start was to provide young children (mainly 4-year-olds) with social and cognitive competence by addressing certain specific outcomes felt to increase the likelihood that students would succeed when they entered elementary school. It was designed to achieve these outcomes through seven service components: education, parent involvement, mental health, physical health, nutrition, social services, and disabled student services or special needs.

Head Start has served millions of children since its inception in 1965, and its effects have been extensively evaluated. Like Title I, Head Start is a funding source, not a specific program. Thus it is difficult to evaluate Head Start as a whole, as many different Head Start centers have different curriculum goals. Studies have shown that overall, the program is effective in helping children to adjust to kindergarten and elementary school (McKey et al., 1985), in including parents as participants in their children's education, and in seeing that children are up to date on their immunizations.

Karweit (1989, 1994) and Stein, Leinhardt, and Bickel (1989) reviewed the effects of Head Start programs, and their syntheses found that Head Start showed immediate improvement on cognitive functioning (ES = +.52). After the first year, the effects decreased substantially (ES = +.10), and decreased further during the second and third years (ES = +.08 and +.02, respectively). Longitudinal studies of the Perry Preschool program, described below, have found positive effects of preschool participation on such outcomes as high graduation and delinquency, but there is little indication at any age that attending Head Start or other early childhood programs increases performance on measures of school achievement, such as reading or math scores.

Perry Preschool–High/Scope

One of the most extensively researched curriculum-specific early childhood education programs is the Perry Preschool curriculum (Weikart, Rogers, Adcock, & McClelland, 1971). The creators of the Perry Preschool curriculum believe in empowering the family, the child, and the teacher, as in Head Start programs, but the Perry Preschool program also has specific academic goals for participants in the program, and its developers created a specific curriculum to accomplish these goals. Based on Piaget's theories of cognition, the Perry Preschool curriculum seeks to increase academic achievement and reduce students' chances of being placed in special education classes by teaching them to become active learners. The teacher acts as a facilitator of knowledge who sets up the classroom in such a way that the student is provided with the opportunity to learn math, science, reading, art, music, social studies, and movement every day. Students choose what they wish to study or work with, but the teacher is expected to be available to answer any questions and clarify any misunderstandings that students may have.

The Perry Preschool model has been evaluated to investigate both short-term and long-term outcomes with at-risk preschoolers. As with other preschool programs, the Perry Preschool program has shown immediate (end of the year) positive effects on cognitive measures such as IQ, but these effects do not maintain into elementary school.

In addition to the cognitive gains made by students who had

attended Perry Preschool programs, a longitudinal evaluation of the effects of the Perry Preschool program on at-risk students (Schweinhart & Weikart, 1980; Schweinhart, Weikart, & Larner, 1986a, 1986b) showed that children involved in these programs tended to stay in school longer, had fewer cases of teenage pregnancies and juvenile arrests, were retained less, were less likely to drop out of school, were more literate, were more likely to be employed, and were more likely to attend college or vocational school than students in control groups who had had no preschool experience. Evaluations of the long-term effects of the program on social adjustment showed that when students in three preschool groups (Direct Instruction, High/Scope, and nursery) were compared on self-reported delinquency, High/Scope students were less likely to have committed delinquent acts, followed by students who had attended traditional nursery school, and followed by students involved in Direct Instruction.

A 22-year follow-up study done on 95% of the participants involved in the original High/Scope study (Schweinhart, Barnes, & Weikart, 1993) showed that High/Scope graduates still had a smaller chance of being arrested than the control group (35%), earned approximately $2,000 per month more than non-program members, were more likely to own their own home (36%) than non-program participants (13%), and had a higher rate of high school graduation (71%) than the control group students (54%).

The High/Scope curriculum exists today in all 50 states. The program also provides an early elementary curriculum that is used around the nation.

Early Intervention for School Success (EISS)

Project Early Intervention for School Success (EISS; *Early Intervention for School Success*, 1986; Rogers, 1993) is an early intervention program developed under special funding from the California Legislature to provide low-income children with early education opportunities to help them become successful learners and thinkers. The legislative intent of this program was threefold: first, to establish a system to identify pupils at the ages of 4 to 7 who may be at risk; second, to implement appropriate instructional programs to reduce the frequency and severity of learning disability for these pupils in later years; and third, to reduce the likelihood that these pupils will be placed in remedial programs with higher costs. Specific learning areas that this program strives to improve include receptive language, visual motor skills, and academic achievement.

EISS works with early childhood providers in California to teach them effective ways to educate children by training them to use developmentally appropriate curricula. Specifically, the teachers are trained in organization and planning, assessment, strategies, and curriculum. The EISS program does not have its own curriculum, but rather it trains teachers to adjust their own curricula so that the children are being taught content that will benefit them academically, linguistically, culturally, and ethnically. EISS facilitators also train the teachers to be sensitive to the cultural and economic backgrounds of the students. Academic goals of the program include improving the children's receptive language and their visual-motor skills.

To date, two studies have evaluated the effectiveness of EISS. In the first study, which compared control and experimental groups, the effects of EISS on receptive language and visual motor skills were evaluated. The students in the treatment group received the EISS curriculum for a period of 7.2 months between pre- and posttesting. EISS students outperformed the control group on the Peabody Picture Vocabulary Test (PPVT), with effect sizes of +.31 in 1989-1990 and +.29 in 1990-1991. Visual motor skills, which were measured using the Visual Motor Integrated test (VMI), produced similar outcomes in favor of EISS students, with an effect size of +.50 in 1990-1991.

To evaluate the long-term academic achievement effects of EISS on both English- and Spanish-speaking children, a number of different tests were used. The Comprehensive Test of Basic Skills (CTBS-4) and the Stanford Achievement Test (SAT-8) were used for the English-speaking children, and the Aprenda Spanish Achievement Test was used for the Spanish-speaking children who had received EISS in kindergarten during the 1989-1990 academic year. When compared to a matched non–EISS group, students maintained large gains (ES = +1.09) the first year after the program, and medium gains (ES = +.65) after being out of the program for 2 years.

EISS also performed a longitudinal study (*Early Intervention for School Success*, 1995) to investigate the long-term effects of the program on achievement, the number of special education place-ments, and grade retention. This study included 5,095 students in EISS and 6,333 matched students in control schools. Students in the control groups showed a decrease in retention, but not to the same extent as the EISS group, compared to the 2 years before EISS implementation. Observations in the long-term study show that EISS students were retained at a lower rate than the compari-son students, the lower rates were sustained through third grade, and significantly fewer students were placed in special education classes by the third or fourth grade.

EISS was recognized as an exemplary program by the National Diffusion Network in 1994 and has served approximately 270,000 students in more than 500 schools in California.

Tutoring Programs

Reading Recovery/Descubriendo La Lectura

Reading Recovery (RR) was developed in the mid-1970s by New Zealand educator and psychologist Marie M. Clay (1985), who conducted observational research in the mid-1960s that enabled her to design techniques for detecting and intervening with early reading difficulties of children. During the 1988-1989 aca-demic year, RR was introduced to the United States by researchers at Ohio State University, who had previously received training in New Zealand (Pinnell, DeFord, & Lyons, 1988).

Reading Recovery is an early intervention tutoring program for young readers who are experiencing difficulty in their first year of reading instruction. RR serves the lowest-achieving readers (lowest 20%) in first-grade classes by providing the children with supplemental tutoring in addition to their regular reading classes. Children participating in RR receive daily one-to-one 30-minute lessons for 12 to 20 weeks with a teacher trained in the RR method. The lessons consist of a variety of experiences designed to help children develop effective strategies for reading and writing. When the student reaches a stage at which he or she is able to read at or above the average class level and can continue to read without later remedial help, the student is discontinued from the program. Students who are not discontinued are excluded from the program after 60 lessons and may be placed either in special education classes or in some other form of remedial education.

RR tutors are certified teachers, who receive an additional year's training in Reading Recovery tutoring. The tutoring model emphasizes "learning to read by reading" (Pinnell, 1989; Pinnell et al., 1988). The lessons are one-to-one tutorial sessions that include reading known stories, reading a story that was read once the day before, writing a story, working with a cut-up sentence, and reading a new book. RR does not have a prescribed set of books that each child must read, but teachers involved in the program use a variety of books appropriate to children's reading levels that the children select as they work on the various components of RR. For the first few tutoring sessions, the teacher and student "roam around the known," reading and writing together in an unstructured, supportive fashion, to build a positive relationship and to give the teacher a broader knowledge of the child and his or her reading skills. After this, the teachers begin to use a structured sequence of activities that include rereading familiar books, analysis of student progress, reading and writing of short messages, and reading new books.

Descubriendo La Lectura (DLL) is a Spanish adaptation of Reading Recovery, developed and studied in Tucson, Arizona. It is equivalent in all major program aspects to the original program. Students in Spanish bilingual classes whose reading scores fall at the bottom 20% in the first grade are placed in DLL.

The Ohio State group has conducted three longitudinal studies comparing English Reading Recovery to traditional Title I pull-out or in-class methods. The first (pilot) study (Huck & Pinnell, 1986, Pinnell, 1988) of RR involved first grade students from six inner-city Columbus, Ohio schools and six matched comparison classes. The lowest 20% of students in each class served as the experimental and control group, respectively. The second longitudinal study (DeFord, Pinnell, Lyons, & Young, 1988; Pinnell, Short, Lyons, & Young, 1986) involved 32 teachers in 12 schools in Columbus. Again, students in the lowest 20% of their classes were randomly assigned to Reading Recovery or control conditions. Results showed that Reading Recovery students substantially outperformed control students on almost all measures in a series of assessments developed by the program, except tests of letter identification and word recognition, both of which had ceiling effects. With the exception of these, the effects ranged from +.57 to +.72.

An oral reading measure called Text Reading Level was given at the end of first, second, and third grades. On this test, students were asked to read books that got progressively more difficult. The results of this study for Text Reading Level at the end of first grade showed substantial positive effects for both the pilot cohort and the second cohort (ES = +.72 and +.78, respectively). On a follow-up assessment at the end of second grade, the effects diminished (ES = +.29 and +.46, respectively). At the end of third grade, the effect sizes had diminished even further (ES = +.14 and +.25, respectively). The raw experimental-control differences remained about the same during the 3-year period, but due to the increasing standard deviations the effect sizes diminished (see Wasik & Slavin, 1993).

A third study of Reading Recovery involved schools in 10 districts throughout the state of Ohio (Pinnell et al., 1994). This study compared Reading Recovery to three program variations and a control group. On midyear assessments, Reading Recovery students scored better than control students and better than an RR variation that involved a shorter training period, a group (not one-to-one) version of RR, and an alternative tutoring model. A Gates-McGinitie given in May of first grade showed small and nonsignificant effects, but the following fall RR students scored significantly higher than controls on both Text Reading Level and a dictation test. None of the RR variations were significantly higher than control groups on these measures.

Studies of Reading Recovery conducted by researchers who are not associated with the program find patterns of results similar to those found by the Ohio State researchers. Tests given immediately after the Reading Recovery intervention show substantial positive effects of the program. These effects diminish in size in years after first grade, although some difference is usually still detectable in third grade (Baenen, Bernholc, Dulaney, Banks, & Willoughby, 1995; Center, Wheldall, Freeman, Outhred, & McNaught, 1995; Shanahan & Barr, 1995).

An evaluation of DLL was conducted by Escamilla (1994) in Tucson. The experiment compared 23 DLL students to 23 matched comparison students in a school that did not have DLL. In both cases, students were identified as being in the lowest 20% of their classes based on individually administered tests and teacher judgment.

The outcomes of DLL on Spanish reading measures given at the end of first grade were extremely positive. On six scales of a Spanish observation survey adapted from the measures used in evaluations of the English Reading Recovery program, DLL students started out below controls and ended the year substantially ahead of them, with effect sizes (adjusted for pretest differences) ranging from +0.97 to +1.71. These scores were also compared to those of a random sample of all students, most of whom were not having reading difficulties, and the DLL students performed above the level of the classes as a whole on all scales. Students were also pre- and posttested on a standardized test, the Aprenda Spanish Achievement Test. On a total reading score, DLL students increased from the 28th to the 41st percentile. Control students increased from the 26th to the 28th percentile, whereas classes as a whole decreased from the 35th to the 31st percentile.

A much larger study of DLL was carried out in California by Kelly, Gomez-Valdez, Klein, and Neal (1995). This study did not have a low-achieving control group but did show both that "discontinuation rates" (an indicator of successful program completion) were similar in DLL and in English Reading Recovery and that end-of-first-grade reading performance of children who participated in DLL was not far below the level of children in general in their schools (most of whom were not at risk for reading failure).

Reading Recovery is very widely used and has regional training centers in 18 states, mostly at universities. The training or residency period for RR lasts one academic year. Teachers then return to their individual sites to implement the program, staying in contact with the RR network through conferences, newsletters, and other network activities. An estimated 80,000 children in 48 states are being served in the 1994-1995 academic year by Reading Recovery educators.

Summary of Outcomes

As noted earlier, an ideal program for this review would be one that had been rigorously evaluated many times in elementary or secondary schools and had been extensively replicated. However, few programs would meet all of these criteria. Table 3.1 summarizes

TABLE 3.1 Categorization of Classroom Instructional Programs Reviewed

Program Name	Grades Served	Meets Evaluation Criteria for Achievement?	Widely Replicated?
Cooperative Learning Methods			
CIRC/BCIRC	2-8	Yes	Yes
Complex Instruction/ Finding Out/ Descubrimiento	1-6	Partially	Yes
STAD/TGT	2-12	Yes	Yes
Jigsaw	2-12	Partially	Yes
Learning Together	K-12	Partially	Yes
Reading/Writing/Language Arts Programs			
ECRI	1-10	Yes	Yes
Reciprocal Teaching	1-8	Yes	Yes
Profile Approach to Writing (PAW)	3-12	Yes	Yes
Multi-Cultural Reading and Thinking (McRAT)	3-8	Yes	Yes
Mathematics Programs			
Comprehensive School Mathematics Program	K-6	Yes	Yes
Cognitively Guided Instruction	1	Yes	Yes
Project SEED	3-8	Yes	Yes
Skills Reinforcement Project	3-8	Yes	no
Maneuvers With Mathematics	5-8	Yes	Yes
Early Childhood Programs			
Perry Preschool– High/Scope	Pre-K	Yes	Yes
EISS	Pre-K–1	Yes	Yes
Tutoring Programs			
Reading Recovery/DLL	1	Yes	Yes

the degree to which each of the programs reviewed met the various inclusion criteria. The table is only a summary; see the program reviews or Fashola and Slavin (1997) for more detail on the characteristics, evaluation evidence, and replicability of each program.

What Factors Contribute to Program Effectiveness?

The programs reviewed in this chapter and the previous one vary in focus, research designs, measures, and other aspects, and often serve different populations. In addition, we focused on locating programs that have evidence of effectiveness. Those we found that did not meet our effectiveness criteria typically lacked adequate research designs; rarely do we have evidence that a given program was not effective, as such evidence is seldom reported. For these reasons we cannot definitely compare effective and ineffective programs and reach firm conclusions about what factors contribute to program success. However, in the course of reviewing hundreds of articles for this and other papers on effective programs for students placed at risk, we have identified a set of conditions that are usually present in programs that work. These are discussed below.

1. *Effective programs have clear goals, emphasize methods and materials linked to those goals, and constantly assess students' progress toward the goals.* There is no magic in educational innovation. Programs that work almost invariably have a small set of very well-specified goals (e.g., raise mathematics achievement, improve creative writing skills), a clear set of procedures and materials linked to those goals, and frequent assessments that indicate whether or not the students are reaching the goals. Effective programs leave little to chance. They incorporate many elements, such as research-based curricula, instructional methods, classroom management methods, assessments, and means of helping students who are struggling, all of which are tied in a coordinated fashion to the instructional goals. Programs almost always have their strongest impacts on the objectives they emphasize. For example, programs emphasizing complex problem solving in mathematics report stronger impacts on problem solving than on computations; programs emphasizing thinking skills tend to show effects on thinking skills, not reading comprehension. Again, there is no magic in educational innovation.

Interventions that are not closely linked to desired outcomes rarely affect these outcomes.

2. *Effective and replicable programs have well-specified components, materials, and professional development procedures.* There is a belief in many quarters that each school staff must develop or codevelop their own reform model, that externally developed programs cannot be successfully replicated in schools that had no hand in developing them. This belief is often traced to the influential Rand Change Agent Study, although that study's principal author, Milbrey McLaughlin (1990), later denied that the Change Agent Study in fact implied that externally developed programs could not work in new schools. In fact, over time evidence has mounted that reform models that ask teachers to develop their own materials and approaches are rarely implemented at all (see, e.g., Elmore, 1996; Muncey & McQuillan, 1996). Studies of alternative programs implemented under similar conditions find that the more highly structured and focused programs that provide specific materials and training are more likely to be implemented and effective than are less-well-specified models (e.g. Bodilly, 1996; Herman & Stringfield, 1995).

Within the present review, the same observations hold true. Although there are examples of success in models lacking clear structure, the programs with the most consistent positive effects with at-risk students are those that have definite procedures and materials used in all participating schools. School staffs may be asked to adapt materials to their own needs, and most successful programs have some buy-in procedure to ensure that participating teachers or whole school staffs have made an informed and uncoerced choice to use a given program. The provision of well-specified methods and materials clearly contributes to both the effectiveness of programs and to the ease of replicating programs in additional schools and producing positive outcomes beyond initial pilots.

3. *Effective programs provide extensive professional development.* A characteristic shared by almost all of the effective programs we identified is the provision of extensive professional development and follow-up technical assistance. Few, if any, provide the classic half-day, one-time workshops that constitute the great majority of "inservice" programs, especially those usually provided with text-

book adoptions. On the contrary, most of the successful programs we identified provide many days of inservice followed by in-class technical assistance to give teachers detailed feedback on their program implementations. Typically, teachers work with each other and with peer or expert coaches to discuss, assess, and refine their implementations. The training provided is rarely on generic strategies from which teachers pick a few ideas to add to their bags of tricks. Instead, training focuses on comprehensive strategies that replace, not just supplement, teacher's current strategies.

4. *Effective programs are disseminated by organizations that focus on the quality of implementation.* The programs identified in this review that have been associated with consistent positive effects in many settings tend to be ones that are developed and disseminated by active, well-structured organizations that concentrate efforts on ensuring the quality of program implementation in all schools. These organizations, often based in universities, provide training and materials and typically create support networks among program users. For example, many of the organizations have national and/or regional conferences to keep up participants' skills and commitment, distribute newsletters and other updates, and work to ensure that schools claiming to use the program are in fact doing so with adequate preparation and integrity. Few of the programs are distributed by commercial publishers.

Note

1. This chapter is adapted from Fashola and Slavin (1997).

4

Dropout Prevention and College Attendance Programs[1]

A high school diploma is the minimum qualification for full participation in the U.S. economy. A worker without one can find work in only the most menial of occupations. The factory jobs that once allowed workers to make good incomes without a high school degree are diminishing, and the educational requirements for jobs in general are increasing. High school dropouts are seriously at risk. For example, they are four times more likely than high school graduates to be on welfare; 27% of dropouts, but only 6% of high school graduates who did not attend college, are on welfare (Educational Testing Service, [ETS], 1995; National Center for Education Statistics [NCES], 1996). Unemployment for workers over age 19 is twice as high for dropouts than for graduates (NCES, 1996; Rumberger, 1987; Stern, Paik, Caterall, & Nakata, 1989).

For most segments of the U.S. population, high school graduation rates have been steadily increasing during the past two decades. Between 1972 and 1994, the white, non-Latino drop-out rate (individuals aged 16 to 24 out of school without a degree) has diminished by more than a third, from 12.3% to 7.7%. The African American drop-out rate has diminished by more than 40%, from 21.3% to 12.6%. In contrast, the drop-out rate among Latino students has always been high and has only slightly diminished. It was 34.3% in 1972, and 30.0% in 1994 (NCES, 1993, 1996). Yet, among all minority groups, drop-out rates remain higher than they should be. Furthermore, among high school graduates, college attendance rates are too low for minority students. Minority and other low-income students are much less likely than middle-class students to attend college (NCES, 1995).

During the past 10 years, a number of programs designed to affect drop-out rates and college attendance have been implemented and evaluated in middle and high schools serving many students placed at risk. Collectively, these studies show that schools can make a dramatic difference in the drop-out rates, school success, and college enrollment rates of at-risk youth. The purpose of this chapter is to review research on programs of this kind.

Dropout Prevention Approaches

There are many quite different approaches to dropout prevention, which are often used in combination or with different subgroups in the same schools. One approach is primary prevention, providing students with high-quality elementary and middle school experiences to deal with the key precursors to dropout, low achievement, retention in grade, dislike of school, and related outcomes. Of course, improving student performance is of value in its own right, but as a dropout prevention strategy increasing school success at all levels is obviously important (Ekstrom, Goertz, Pollack, & Rock, 1986; Finn, 1989). Increasing the quality and attractiveness of the secondary curriculum is another obvious approach to dropout prevention. Secondary whole-school reforms intended to improve the achievement and social development of adolescents would be expected to affect drop-out rates as well. However, even with the best preventive programs, many students will still be at risk for dropout, and many will fail to achieve their full potential. Interventions are needed in secondary schools to increase the chances that students will stay in school, complete their high school degrees, and make a successful transition to post-secondary studies or to the workforce.

Other approaches to dropout prevention focus on identifying key hurdles to school success and helping students over them. For example, many approaches provide individual or small group tutoring to help students pass courses, especially such critical "gatekeeper" courses as algebra and English. After school, summer school, and Saturday programs are often provided to help students make it through their coursework (see, for example, Rumberger & Larson, 1994). Recognizing the strong correlation between truancy and dropout, many programs also focus on increasing student attendance.

A recurrent theme in many dropout prevention programs is the importance of personalizing the high school experience for at-risk students, with an expectation that increasing attachments to valued adults in the school or giving students high-status roles in the school will reduce disaffection and dropout. Various mentoring or counseling programs are built around this theme, as is the approach taken in at least a few programs of engaging young adolescents in prosocial activities such as tutoring younger children or volunteering in nursing homes.

Another theme in many dropout prevention programs is giving students a sense of purpose for completing school, in essence making the long-term consequences of high school completion and college attendance more apparent on a day-to-day basis. For example, many dropout prevention programs have a strong link to vocational education, part-time job placements, and internships in local businesses, both to maintain students' interests in school and to give them a clear picture of what life after school might be like and how a diploma helps in the real world (see Hayward & Tallmadge, 1995). Similarly, many programs designed to increase college attendance, including the widely used Upward Bound model, place students on college campuses during the summer to give them a realistic idea of what college life is like and a more concrete experience of a potential future. An important variant of this approach involves providing college scholarships to students who meet certain standards of performance in high school.

Focus of the Review

The focus of this review is on the identification of programs that have been shown to have a significant impact on dropouts, college attendance, school performance, or related outcomes in rigorous evaluations that are replicable across a broad range of secondary schools and that have been successfully evaluated among students placed at risk. As in the other chapters in this book, we apply consistent standards to evaluate the likely effectiveness and replicability of programs available to educators committed to transforming secondary schools and classrooms to meet the students' diverse needs.

Selection for Review

Ideally, programs emphasized in this review would be those that present rigorous evaluation evidence in comparison to control groups showing significant and lasting impacts on dropout or related outcomes, have active dissemination programs that have implemented the program in many schools, and have evidence of effectiveness in dissemination sites, ideally from studies conducted by third parties. To require all of these conditions, however, would limit this review to just two programs (Upward Bound and the Coca-Cola Valued Youth Project). As in other chapters, we have had to compromise on one or more criteria.

Programs that are not discussed are ones that have less than convincing evidence of effectiveness and are not widely replicated. For example, a set of evaluations of dropout prevention programs summarized by Rossi (1996) had many methodological problems, especially involving poor matching between experimental and control schools, and the programs themselves were designed for individual schools or districts and lacked training staffs capable of introducing the programs to other districts. Similarly, studies of dropout prevention programs by Edgar and Johnson (1995) and Sinclair, Thurlow, Christenson, and Evelo (1995) both produced uneven outcomes and were not replicated beyond their original districts.

Following detailed discussions of the programs and their evaluations, Table 4.1 summarizes the degree to which each program reviewed meets our ideal criteria. We have tried to present the evidence that school and district staff would need to begin a process leading to an informed choice from among effective and promising programs capable of being replicated in their settings.

Program Types

Six programs met the inclusion criteria included in this review. These programs (as well as many others that did not meet our standards) fall into two major categories. The first is programs designed to work with the most at-risk students in middle, junior high, or high school to keep them from dropping out. The second category is programs designed to increase the college attendance rates (or college eligibility) of students who may show promise but are at risk of not fulfilling their promise. The college attendance programs also emphasize dropout prevention as a goal, and programs designed strictly as dropout prevention models often report college attendance or eligibility as a valued outcome, but there is a clear distinction in practice between the two types of programs in terms of their emphasis on helping students to take and pass courses that lead to college, familiarizing students with college, assisting students with financial aid applications, and in one case (Project GRAD) actually providing college scholarships.

Dropout Prevention Programs

Two programs primarily designed to increase the high school graduation rates of at-risk students met the standards of this review: The Coca-Cola Valued Youth Program (VYP) and ALAS (Achievement for Latinos Through Academic Success).

The Coca-Cola Valued Youth Program

The Coca-Cola Valued Youth Program (*Coca-Cola Valued Youth Program*, 1991) is a cross-age tutoring program designed to increase the self-esteem and school success of at-risk middle and high school students by placing them in positions of responsibility as tutors of younger elementary school students. The Valued Youth Program was originally developed by the Intercultural Development Research Association in San Antonio, Texas. The original implementation of the program was funded by Coca-Cola and implemented in collaboration with five school districts in San Antonio between 1984 and 1988, with approximately 525 high school tutors and 1575 elementary tutees.

The overall goal of the program is to reduce the drop-out rates of at-risk students by improving their self-concepts and academic skills. This is done by making them tutors and providing assistance with basic academic skills. The program also emphasizes elimination of nonacademic and disciplinary factors that contribute to dropping out. For example, it attempts to develop students' sense of self-control, decrease student truancy, and reduce disciplinary referrals. It also seeks to form home-school partnerships to increase the level of support available to students.

The first goals of improvement of academic skills is met when students agree to serve as tutors. The tutors are required to enroll in a special tutoring class, which allows them to improve their own basic academic skills as well as their tutoring skills. The students who are involved as tutors are paid a minimum wage stipend. The tutors work with three elementary students at a time for a total of about 4 hours per week. They are taught to develop self-awareness and pride, which is expected to make them less likely to exhibit disciplinary problems.

Functions are held to honor and recognize the tutors as role models. They receive T-shirts, caps, and certificates of merit for their efforts.

The main evaluation of the Coca-Cola Valued Youth Program compared 63 VYP tutors to 70 students in a comparison group (Cardenas, Montecel, Supik, & Harris, 1992). The students in four San Antonio schools were matched on the basis of age; ethnicity; lunch eligibility; percentage of students retained in grade; and scores on tests of reading, quality of school life, and self-concept. They were selected (not randomly) into the experimental group based on scheduling and availability, and then the remaining students were placed into the comparison group. Nearly all students in both groups were Latino and limited English proficient. The control students were somewhat less likely to qualify for free lunch or to have been retained in grade.

Two years after the program began, 12% of the comparison students but only 1% of the VYP students had dropped out. Reading grades were significantly higher for the VYP group, as were scores on a self-esteem measure and on a measure of attitude towards school.

The VYP has been widely replicated throughout the Southwest and elsewhere. In 1990, additional funding was provided by Coca-Cola for sites in California, Florida, New York, and Texas, and the program is now being extended to schools in Idaho, Oregon, Montana, and other schools across the country.

Achievement for Latinos
Through Academic Success (ALAS)

ALAS (Larson & Rumberger, 1995) is a dropout prevention program for high-risk middle or junior high school Latino students, particularly Mexican American students from high-poverty neighborhoods. This program focuses on youth with learning and emotional/behavioral disabilities using a collaborative approach across multiple spheres of influence: home, school, and community.

Students served in the program came from primarily Latino Los Angeles communities in neighborhoods with high rates of crime, drug use, and gang activity.

The intervention addressed three major forces that influence the life of the adolescent: family, community, and school. Students were provided with social problem-solving training, counseling, and recognition for academic excellence. School strategies included remediating the students' deficient social and task-related problem-solving skills, maintaining intensive attendance monitoring, providing recognition and bonding activities for the participants, and providing frequent teacher feedback to the parent and the student. Family strategies included use of community resources, parent training in school participation, and training to guide and monitor adolescents. Parents were offered workshops on school participation and teen behavior management. The program also focused on integrating school and home needs with community services and advocating for the student and parent when necessary. Community strategies included enhancement of collaboration among community agencies for youth and family services, and enhancement of skills and methods for serving the youth and family.

ALAS was evaluated in a junior high school that was 96% Latino with 70% of the students in the school participating in the school lunch program. Of the cohort of students who entered the seventh grade in 1990, 62% spoke English as a first language; 60% remained in school for Grades 7, 8, and 9; and only 65% of these students had earned enough high school credits in the ninth grade.

ALAS served the most at-risk students in the school. Students who fit this category were identified in one of two ways. One group of students had had an active Individualized Education Plan (IEP) from sixth grade, identifying them as learning disabled or severely emotionally disabled using state and federal guidelines.

These students are referred to as the Special Education (SE) group. Students with IEPs who entered the seventh grade during fall of 1990 (the first year of implementation) were placed in the special education treatment group 1 (SE1, $n = 33$). Students with IEPs who entered the seventh grade during fall of 1991 (the second year of implementation) were placed in the special education treatment group 2 (SE2, $n = 44$). Students with IEPs who entered the seventh grade during the third year of the study were placed in the special education control group (SEC, $n = 55$).

Students in the second category were those who were not formally identified for special education but who exhibited characteristics that placed them at risk for dropping out of school. These students were identified using a six-item teacher rating scale that evaluated students' level of functioning based upon level of motivation, academic potential, social interaction skill, difficulty to teach, and need for special education services. Students in this group were classified as High Risk (HR) if they rated below average on 4 or more of the 6 categories. Students who spoke no English were excluded from the study. Students who qualified as high risk were randomly assigned to one of two groups. The first group of at-risk students consisted of the high-risk seventh-grade students who entered the seventh grade in the fall of 1990 and received the ALAS treatment (HRT; $n = 46$). The second group consisted of the high-risk seventh-grade students who did not receive the ALAS treatment, but served as a control group (HRC; $n = 48$). A low-risk group was also assessed to provide an additional point of comparison. This group of students fit the demographic descriptions of students receiving ALAS.

The full impact of the program was not supposed to have taken effect until the children had been in the program for at least 2 years. Results were reported at the end of the 9th grade, and follow-up assessment was done at the end of the 11th grade.

In this study, "dropout" was defined as not being enrolled in school during the last 20 days of ninth grade, with no requests for student records from another school. Among the special education samples, the second cohort (SE2) had the lowest drop-out rate (2%). This was significantly lower than the other two groups. The first special education cohort (SE1) experienced a 12% drop-out rate, and although this was less than the drop-out rate for the special education control group (16%), the difference was not statistically significant.

Among the high-risk groups, the ALAS students had a much lower drop-out rate (2.2%) than the high-risk control group (16.7%). The rate for the high-risk treatment group was even lower than that for the low-risk comparison group (5.1%). In summary, the ALAS program worked well for the students in the treatment groups, and especially well for students in the second special education cohort and the high-risk group. The attrition rates (dropouts plus transfers to other schools) were also lower for the treatment groups than they were for the control groups.

Another variable measured was the number of high school credits earned by the students in the various groups, defined as accumulating enough units by the end of the ninth grade (including summer) to be on track to graduate from high school in 4 or 5 years.

Among the special education cohorts, 54% of the first cohort and 70% of the second cohort had accumulated enough units to graduate, compared to 30% of the special education control group. More of the low-risk students (70%) earned their high school credits than any of the at-risk groups. More of the high-risk treatment (56%) students than the high-risk control (45%) students had enough credits.

ALAS also measured recovery rates as the percentage of students who left the school who then returned. This was another measure of the "holding power" of the ALAS program. Students with the highest recovery rates were those in the treatment groups. Special education cohort 1 (SE1) had a 47% recovery rate, whereas special education cohort 2 (SE2) had a 33% recovery rate. The special education control group had a 4% recovery rate. The high-risk treatment (HRT) group had a 41% recovery rate, the high-risk control group had a 4% recovery rate, and the low-risk control group had a 21% recovery rate.

Attendance was measured as the percent of students absent more than 25% of the time. Among the special education groups, SE1 had slightly fewer students with more absences (40%) than the SEC (43%), but this difference was not significant. The second special education cohort had significantly fewer students with many absences (19%) than either of the other special education groups. The high-risk treatment group had a lower (15%) absenteeism rate than the high-risk control group (38%).

Another measure of academic progress was the percentage of Fs received by the students in six classes in all of the groups. At the end of the ninth grade, the smallest average percentage of failures occurred among the SE2 group (7.3%), followed closely by the SE1 students (8.25%), and then the high-risk treatment group (8.62%). The two control groups had substantially higher numbers of failures (19.24% for HRC and 20.25% for SEC).

In summary, the groups that benefited the most from ALAS through the end of the ninth grade were the special education second cohort and the high-risk treatment group.

A long-term evaluation of some of the study variables was also done on the initial ALAS cohorts, including the special education cohort 1 (SE1), the high-risk treatment cohort (HRT), the high-risk control group (HRC), and the low-risk control group (LRC).

The first variable followed was the number of high school credits earned by the students. By the 11th grade, although students in the two treatment groups (SE1 and HRT) had more credits than those in the high-risk control group, this difference was not significant, and all had fewer credits than the low-risk control group. Comparing the high-risk treatment and the high-risk control students in terms of whether they had sufficient credits to graduate in 1 or 2 years, the high-risk treatment group had more students qualifying in both cases (33% compared to 25.9% were on track to graduate in no more than 1 year, and 66.7% compared to 51.9% were on track to graduate in no more than 2 years). However, the differences between the two groups were not significant.

ALAS has not been disseminated beyond its pilot sites but provides one effective and well-evaluated model for increasing the school successes and persistence of at-risk Latino students.

College Attendance Programs

Four programs designed to increase the college attendance rates of low-income and minority students met the standards of this review: Upward Bound (UB), SCORE, AVID, and GRAD. In each of these, reducing dropout and increasing academic achievement (among other outcomes) were also important program goals, but these programs are distinctive in their focus on ensuring that promising low–SES and other minority students do what is necessary to attend college.

Upward Bound/TRIO

The U.S. Department of Education administers a set of six college entrance programs whose main goal is to increase the number of first generation, low-socioeconomic status students attending college by providing them with academic skills and additional resources that they may need in order to make them college eligible. The programs, collectively referred to as TRIO, include Upward Bound, Talent Search, Student Support Services, Educational Opportunity Centers, Training Program for Special Services Staff and Leadership Personnel, and the Ronald McNair Post-Baccalaureate Achievement program.

Upward Bound is the oldest and largest of the TRIO programs, and it has been evaluated the most thoroughly. Upward Bound targets 13- to 19-year-old students whose family income is under 150% of the poverty level, and/or students who are potential first generation college entrants. To be eligible for Upward Bound, students must have completed the eighth grade, met the socioeconomic criteria, and plan to attend college. Students are usually recommended into the program by a guidance or academic counselor. Students with behavioral and emotional problems are usually screened out of the pool of applicants.

Once enrolled in Upward Bound, students are provided with extra instruction, usually after school and on Saturdays, in mathematics, laboratory science, foreign language, English, and composition, and are also provided with instruction in study skills, academic or personal counseling, exposure to cultural events, tutorial services, information about financial assistance opportunities in college, and advice on a range of career options. The most important element of the program is an intensive 6-week summer academic residential or nonresidential program at a college campus.

The first comprehensive evaluation of Upward Bound was done by Burkheimer, Levinsohn, Koo, and French (1976) and followed up by Burkheimer, Riccobono, and Wisenbaker (1979). This evaluation investigated the high school retention rates of UB students, the rate of entry of UB students into postsecondary institutions, and Upward Bound's effectiveness in helping students to attain skills and motivation necessary for postsecondary success.

The experimental design consisted of matched comparison groups, comparing 3,710 UB students and 2,340 comparison students in the 10th, 11th, and 12th grades who attended the same schools. Students in the two groups were matched on grade level, ethnicity, low-income status, and academic-risk status. Data were collected using questionnaires, interviews, and student records.

Based on fall-to-spring high school continuance rates, UB participants remained in high school at a rate slightly higher than that of the comparison group students. The difference was significant in the 10th and 11th grades, but not 12th. Evidence also suggested that the longer the students were involved in the program, the higher their rate of school continuance. Fall-to-fall high school continuance rates were lower for both groups, but the UB students still showed a higher continuation rate in Grade 10, but not in Grades 11 or 12.

The UB students entered institutions of post secondary education (PSE) at a higher rate than the comparison students. UB had a greater percentage of high school graduates who were eligible to attend college (71%) than did the comparison group (47%), and 65% of the college eligible UB students attended PSE institutions versus 43% of the control group.

UB students involved in the program the longest benefited the most from the program. Students who had participated in UB for 3 years had a 78% college attendance rate; those who had participated in UB for 2 years had a 69% college attendance rate; and those who had participated for 1 year had a 68% college attendance rate.

The most recent evaluation of Upward Bound was done by Mathematica Policy Research, Inc. (MPR). This evaluation has produced an initial report focusing on the short-term academic impact of UB on students during the first 2 years of high school. Secondary questions answered by the evaluation included the length of students' participation in UB, attrition rates in UB, reasons for leaving the program, what types of students benefited from UB services, and the types of services provided by UB.

A pool of potential participants was collected by asking students across the country to complete UB applications and also to complete a questionnaire that asked about family background, attitudes and expectations, and school experiences. A follow-up survey updated their school-related experiences, attitudes, and expectations. Data from high school transcripts were also used in the selection process. Eligible participants from 67 sites participating in UB were then selected and randomly assigned to an Upward

Bound group (1,481 students) or a control group (1,266 students).

Overall, the students in this study were mostly female (70%) and African American (53%). Latinos made up 25% of the sample; other participants included Caucasian (12%), Asian (5%), and Native American (5%) students.

Of the students invited to participate in Upward Bound, 20% chose not to join. Many students did not participate in the program because they had taken jobs or had problems with transportation, family issues, or time conflicts. Latino and Asian students were more likely to participate when invited than were African American students, and younger students were also more likely to participate than were older students.

Of the students who joined the program, about 40% failed to complete it. Students who planned to complete less than a baccalaureate degree were more likely to drop out of the program, as were students who took jobs. African American students were more likely to leave UB than members of other ethnic groups.

Analyses of UB showed that the UB participants earned more academic credits during high school, particularly in English, social studies, and science, than the control group. Of the students who remained in the study, UB participants received considerably more academic preparation and support for college than did students in the control group. They were also more likely to take courses such as English, mathematics, and science.

As in the earlier study (Burkheimer et al., 1979), length of time in the program was an important indicator of success. Participants who had been involved in UB for longer periods of time earned more credits in high school than did other students. Grade point averages, attitudes about high school, and parental involvement were not affected by participation in Upward Bound. Students' expectations and attitudes toward future success, however, decreased significantly less than those of the control group, but they decreased nonetheless, whereas their parents' expectations increased. Grade point averages for the two groups remained the same, even though the UB counterparts in the control groups were not required to take academic courses and were less likely to do so than were the UB students. In other words, the Upward Bound students were receiving equivalent grades in more difficult academic courses.

UB students earned more academic credits for their courses in science, mathematics, English, foreign languages, and social studies as well as more vocational education credits and more remedial mathematics credits than did their counterparts. All of these differences were statistically significant.

The impact of UB was greater for Latino students who had entered the program with low expectations than for any of the other student participants. Latino UB participants increased their academic coursework by 2 credits each year; African American and white students increased their academic loads by less than .5 credits. Evidence showed that almost all of the African American and white students, but only 87% of Latino students, would have participated in an academic curriculum regardless of UB.

Examining preliminary long-term results of UB, MPR showed high rates of college entrance, but low rates of student persistence in college. Of the UB students entering college, those with lower expectations of college completion were more likely to drop out.

There are several limitations of the MPR evaluation that tend to understate the impact of Upward Bound. One involved the UB attrition problem (which the program acknowledges). As noted before, 20% of the students selected did not enter the program, and another 40% of those who entered dropped out of it. This means that of all of the students evaluated, only about 50% of the students received the entire 12-month program. Yet all invited students were included in the analyses, no matter how much they participated.

Another limitation of the study is its difficulty in identifying a truly untreated control group. Some of the control group students may have had access to the same or similar types of services as the UB students. The authors state that more than 40% of the students in the control group received similar services, such as Talent Search (which is another TRIO program).

After the initial evaluation of UB (Burkheimer et al., 1979), the program strengthened its academic component and added more enrichment courses to the summer program. Also, at that time, UB existed more at 4-year institutions than at 2-year institutions. Since then, UB has expanded such that there is a significant number of Upward Bound programs at 2-year institutions. However, due to funding problems at the community college level, many 2-year institutions that provide UB services do not offer the 6-week summer program.

Although Upward Bound is funded federally, it is operated at local public and private institutions of higher education, 2 year as well as 4 year. The funding cycle for Upward Bound programs is generally 3 years, although the program is usually continuous at any given site. Upward Bound began in 1967, and it now serves about 42,000 precollegiate students with a budget of $162.5 million.

SCORE

SCORE (Johnson, 1983) is a dropout prevention/college preparatory program that was initially developed as a partnership between the Orange County (CA) Department of Education and the University of California at Irvine. This program targets at-risk students in Grades 9-12 whose likelihood of graduating from high school or enrolling in college is felt to be low by their teachers. SCORE equips its student participants with the tools that they need to stay in high school and to attend college by providing them with a set of comprehensive services. These services can be separated into five components, which are adapted to the needs of each school.

First, students receive professional career counseling from a SCORE guidance counselor, who helps to work through any obstacles preventing them from meeting their professional goals. Second, students receive tutoring in various subjects and instruction in study skills from SCORE teachers. The third component of SCORE focuses on motivation. SCORE students are given opportunities to join various clubs, in which they work together and provide one another with motivational support. Fourth is a parent program that helps parents to support their children's academic success. The final component is a summer academic program, in which students take courses ranging from college preparatory courses to actual college courses to remedial courses. For Latino and other students with limited English proficiency, SCORE focuses on moving students out of separate ESL classes into the mainstream.

Schools that initially intend to implement SCORE attend a 3-day workshop to discuss schoolwide changes that will need to be in place for implementation. Next, study skills teachers are chosen, and they participate in a 2-day workshop, after which the program is adapted to fit the needs of the specific school. At the end of the implementation year, the program is reevaluated to see whatever changes (if any) need to be made for the following year.

The first evaluations of SCORE (Wells, 1981) involved comparing University of California (U.C.) eligibility rates of the first group of SCORE students with those of the state of California. U.C. eligibility rates for SCORE students were 40%, compared to a random sample of high school African American and Latino graduate students surveyed by the California Post-Secondary Education Council (CPEC) of 5.2%. SCORE students also enrolled at a higher rate (41%) in 4-year colleges than did a selected comparison group of minority high school graduates, also surveyed by CPEC (11%). The next portion of this evaluation compared the effects of partial implementation of SCORE to full implementation. Students who received less than all five components of SCORE had a 32% college enrollment rate, whereas those who had had all five components and attended all sessions (especially including the summer institute) had a 56% college enrollment rate. The last part of this comparison included matching 99 SCORE seniors from a school that was 43% Latino with 112 students from a matched control school that also had a 43% Latino population. All (100%) of the SCORE students completed their college requirements, compared to 52% of the students in the comparison sample.

The SCORE program published anecdotal reports on four schools (*SCORE*, 1994). The first school, in Gonzales, California, consisted of 1200 students, of whom 45% were migrant. Prior to adopting SCORE in 1983, 3% of the high school graduates had completed the requirements to enroll in a university. With the adoption of SCORE, the figures steadily increased until they reached 28% in 1990. Migrant students from Gonzales High School enrolled in 4-year colleges and universities at a much higher rate (51%) than the national migrant average (5%). The number of SCORE students enrolled in intermediate algebra also rose from 42 to 119 and from 12 to 63 in other mathematics courses. Chemistry and physics enrollment also increased from 60 in 1987 to 175 in 1992.

The second school, in Madera, CA, was 100% Latino, and all of the students were involved in migrant education. When they initially entered the school, many of the students were limited English proficient. Upon graduation, 93% of the LEP students tested as fully English proficient. After participating in SCORE, 90% of the migrant students who participated attended college. 100% of the students who graduated attended either 4- or 2-year colleges. Some of the students dropped out as a result of financial issues, but none because of academic problems.

Students in a school in Buena Park, CA, who had been selected into SCORE were those who had scored in the bottom quartile on the CTBS, and therefore qualified as Title I students. This group made up 69% of the total freshman class. The percentage of graduates who attended 4-year colleges went up from 22% to 31%. While in college, all of the SCORE graduates maintained a 2.8 GPA in their college prep curriculum during their freshman year. All limited English proficient students were also fully English proficient at the end of the freshman year and maintained a B GPA through their senior year in high school. Buena Park High School eliminated remedial mathematics, instituted algebra for most ninth grade students, and then heterogeneously grouped all social science classes. The drop-out rates decreased from 3.3 to 2.3.

The final school, in Stockton, CA, had a heterogeneous mix of students. Here, SCORE operates mainly as an after-school tutorial program, using teachers who tutor in their classrooms 1 to 4 days per week. Since the adoption of SCORE, elective enrollment in college preparatory classes increased 84% from the previous year. The number of students who took the SAT also increased from 11 in 1982 to 110 in 1993. The number of advanced placement English classes also increased from one to six, and most recently, the school has adopted an international baccalaureate program. The number of students who dropped out decreased from 141 in 1988 to 71 in 1992.

The evaluations of SCORE are far from ideal in experimental design. Most of the statistics presented for SCORE students are anecdotal; different outcomes, presumably those showing the most impressive gains, are reported for each school. The first study compared SCORE students to California averages for minority students, without any evidence that the SCORE students were similar in other ways to California averages. However, the changes over time in drop-out and college enrollment rates are large and have been shown in many schools. It seems likely that SCORE is in fact having an important impact on the graduation and college enrollment rates of at-risk students.

SCORE is currently used in several schools in Southern California and is being expanded through a process of training trainers in new schools and districts.

Project AVID

Project Advancement Via Individual Determination (AVID; Mehan et al., 1992; Swanson, Mehan, & Hubbard, 1995) is a high school college enrollment program that began in San Diego county, California, in 1981. In AVID, low-achieving students felt to have good academic potential are placed in rigorous college prep courses and are taught to excel academically. The program began as a means of improving the academic achievement of minority students who were being bused into a predominantly white suburban high school in San Diego County.

When schools initially agree to become AVID schools, a leadership team made up of the school principal, head counselor, AVID teacher, and the leaders in English, foreign languages, history, science, and mathematics attend a weeklong summer training institute. Follow-up training is also provided in the form of monthly workshops by the AVID lead teachers, semiannual site team meetings and site visitations by the AVID county staff, and quarterly tutor and parent workshops.

The main backbone of the AVID program is the lead teacher/ coordinator. He or she acts as a coach, constantly expecting the best academic performances from both the teachers and the students. The AVID lead teacher/coordinator is also responsible for training and hiring professionals and paraprofessionals such as tutors to work with the students in the program. The lead teachers raise funds for the program, and are involved in the coordination and planning of field trips.

Students who participate in AVID are selected into the program by AVID coordinators. Eligibility requirements include average to high CTBS scores, but low junior high school grades, as well as parental consent. Once the students enter the program they enroll in AVID classes, where they are taught such strategies as inquiry, writing, and higher-order thinking skills. They are also provided academic assistance and tutoring in their regular subjects during the AVID class hours. Sometimes, some of the AVID students themselves are the tutors.

Students participate in AVID activities during lunch, recess, elective periods, and after school. They may be given AVID notebooks that are used to take "AVID-style notes," and AVID badges or ribbons. Some schools engage students in printing a special

AVID newspaper that discusses AVID student successes.

In the most recent evaluation of AVID, Mehan, Villanueva, Hubbard, and Lintz (1996) compared the school records of 248 students who had participated in AVID for 3 years (AVID3) in 1990-1992 with those of 146 students who had also met the criteria for AVID and initially participated in the program for a year, but then dropped out (AVID1). Students' records were from 14 AVID schools in San Diego county, with Latino compositions ranging from 8% to 37%. The original number of students in each group was 353 for the AVID3 students and 288 for the AVID1 students, and the number of Latino students who participated in the follow-up interviews was 102 in the AVID3 group and 40 for the AVID1 group. The two groups were fairly equal in socioeconomic status. Among AVID3 students, 71% came from homes whose families made under $40,000 per annum, as opposed to 65% of the AVID1 students.

Analyses comparing AVID3 and AVID1 divided students into three groups. The first group (high) consisted of students who had high CTBS scores and high grades, or middle CTBS scores and high grades. In this group, there were 37 (25%) AVID1 students and 72 (29%) AVID3 students. The second group (middle) consisted of students who had high CTBS scores and middle-level grades, or middle-level scores and middle-level grades. The middle group consisted of 77 (53%) AVID1 students and 140 (56%) AVID3 students. The final group (low) consisted of students who had both low grades and low CTBS scores. This group consisted of 32 (22%) AVID1 and 36 (15%) AVID3 students.

The college enrollment rates of the two AVID groups were compared to those of the San Diego county high school population and to those of the U.S. population. Comparisons of these four groups showed that AVID students had a greater rate of attending 4-year institutions, followed by AVID1 students. Looking specifically at the Latino students, who comprised the majority of the students in the study, 43% attended 4-year institutions, compared to the San Diego county rate of 25% and the AVID1 rate of 20%. Interestingly, 43% of the AVID3 graduates attended 2-year colleges, compared to 40% of the AVID1 students and 37% of the county population; and 14% of the AVID3 students were engaged in work right after high school, compared to 38% of the county population and 40% of the AVID1 population. Comparing the AVID1 and

AVID3 groups on attempting and actually completing college preparation classes to make them eligible for the University of California or the California State University system, the differences favored the AVID3 group. In the high AVID1 group, 78% of the students attempted college preparation courses and 62% of them completed these courses, compared to the AVID3 group, where 85% of the students attempted the courses and 67% completed them. For the middle students, there was a similar pattern. For the AVID1 middle group, 42% of the students attempted the courses, and 14% of them completed the courses, compared to 68% of the middle AVID3 students who attempted the courses and 23% who actually completed them. The largest impact of participating in this program shows up in the low groups.

For the AVID1 low group, 22% of the students attempted the college level courses and none of them completed the courses, compared to 53% of the low AVID3 students who attempted the courses and 11% who actually completed them.

The advantage of AVID3 over AVID1 participants was greatest for students whose parents had not completed high school (44% for AVID3 versus 17% for AVID1). There was a smaller but still important difference for students whose parents were high school graduates (51% for AVID3 versus 39% for AVID1) and for students whose parents had a bachelor's degree or more (48% for AVID3 versus 39% for AVID1).

Overall, these results suggest that AVID had some positive effects on the students who needed it most. It is important to note that the Mehan et al. (1996) study, although it uses a comparison group, still presents issues of concern, and does not meet the standards of this review. First, the AVID1 and AVID3 groups cannot be considered comparable, as the AVID3 students were able to remain in this rigorous program for all 3 years whereas the AVID1 students dropped out. It is likely that the AVID3 students were therefore more motivated, higher achieving, and better behaved than the AVID1 students. Comparison of both AVID groups to San Diego county and U.S. means are even more susceptible to bias. Students are specially selected for AVID based on high CTBS scores and other indications of promise, and some number of students do not even make it to the end of the first year (and are therefore not included in either group). Still, the college enrollment rates for AVID are impressive, and the program has a good track record in serving students throughout the United States, and for these reasons is worthy of consideration by other schools serving many students placed at risk.

AVID now exists in 50 high schools in San Diego county and 84 high schools outside the county.

Project GRAD

Project GRAD (Graduation Really Achieves Dreams; Ketelsen, 1994) is a comprehensive dropout prevention/college attendance program developed and evaluated at Jefferson Davis High School, which serves a population that is 83% Latino and very low in socioeconomic status. It was begun in 1989 by a former CEO of Tenneco, James Ketelsen, in collaboration with the University of Houston. Tenneco and other funders promised any student who graduated on time from Jefferson Davis with a GPA of 2.5 a 4-year, $1,000-per-year college scholarship. Students were provided with two 5-week summer academic institutes held at the University of Houston, opportunities to participate in paid internships in local businesses, and interventions to improve schoolwide discipline, parent involvement, and quality of instruction. An evaluation of Project GRAD compared the entire school population in 1989, before the program began, with those in 1993 (Ketelsen, 1994). During that time period, the percentage of students graduating in 4 years rose from 50% to 78%. College attendance rose from 10% of all graduates to 60%. The pass rate on the 11th-grade Texas Assessment of Academic Skills (TAAS) increased from 37% to 86%, and the number of students enrolled in honors courses doubled.

A more recent comparison of Project GRAD to a control school (Opuni, 1995) showed less impressive outcomes in terms of graduation rates and academic achievement but continued to show substantial gains in college attendance. Annual drop-out rates at Jefferson Davis dropped from 18% in 1988-1989 to 11.5% in 1994-1995, but similar reductions were also found in the comparison schools and in other Houston high schools. Only small differences (favoring Davis) were found in on-time graduation rates, and there were no differences on academic achievement measures. However, among students who did graduate, college attendance rates increased from 20% in 1988-1989 to 41% who attended college immediately after high school and 56% who eventually did so. This is more

TABLE 4.1   Categorization of Dropout Prevention
             and College Attendance Programs Reviewed

Program Name	Grades Served	Meets Evaluation Criteria for Achievement?	Widely Replicated?
Dropout Prevention			
Coca-Cola Valued Youth Project (VYP)	7-12	Yes	Yes
ALAS	7-12	Yes	No
College Attendance			
Upward Bound	9-12	Yes	Yes
SCORE	9-12	Partially	No
AVID	9-12	Partially	Yes
GRAD	9-12	Yes	No

impressive as the total population of students graduating was also increasing during this time period. Because of the disappointing findings with respect to achievement and dropout, however, the project is adding interventions relating to achievement, discipline, and attendance in the entire feeder system that leads to Davis High (Ketelson, 1994).

At present, Project GRAD only exists at its original site, but there are plans to expand it to additional high schools within and beyond Houston.

Summary of Outcomes

As noted earlier, an ideal program for this review would be one that had been rigorously evaluated many times in middle or high schools serving many students placed at risk, and had been extensively replicated in such schools. However, only Upward Bound and the Coca-Cola Valued Youth Project would meet all of these criteria. Table 4.1 summarizes the degree to which each of the programs reviewed met the various inclusion criteria. The table is only a summary; see the program reviews for more detail on the characteristics, evaluation evidence, and replicability of each program.

Conclusion

The six dropout prevention and college attendance programs that met our evaluation criteria are very diverse in their interventions as well as their findings. Yet there are important commonalities among them as well. First, even accounting for mild to serious problems in experimental design (especially relating to problems of selection bias), it is clear that these programs can have a substantial impact on the drop-out rates, college attendance rates, and other outcomes for adolescents who are placed at risk. Second, although only four of the six (AVID, SCORE, Upward Bound, and the Coca-Cola Valued Youth Program) have active dissemination programs, there is nothing inherent to any of these programs that would keep them from being disseminated broadly. They are expensive, but well within the means of our society, especially given the immediate costs to our society of high drop-out rates and underused talent.

Although the interventions themselves differ considerably, there are some common themes among them. One is personalization, trying to increase the holding power of the school by creating meaningful personal bonds between students and teachers and among students. Most of the programs use some sort of small-group intervention and/or mentoring to enhance individual attachments to school. This addresses several problems that often lead to dropout. One is the depersonalization inherent in departmentalized schools, where one teacher may be responsible for more than 150 students and cannot respond adequately to individuals' needs. A second is the pull of antiacademic forces, such as gangs and other subgroups that disdain or actively oppose academic efforts. Among adolescents who may differ from the mainstream in ethnicity, language, culture, and socioeconomic background, it is easy to fall into a subculture with norms that reject mainstream values. Successful dropout prevention programs often combat this tendency by creating high-status, attractive groups with which students will want to affiliate. Many provide special badges, hats, or other symbols of identification, as well as opportunities for satisfying social interactions with a subgroup composed of students who plan to graduate or to attend college.

Another common element of successful dropout and college attendance programs involves connecting students to an attainable future. For example, both Project GRAD and Upward Bound give students an experience on a college campus to make college seem more real and attainable. SCORE and AVID, among others, provide counseling to help students prepare for college and occupations. Even a bright, academically successful student who comes from a family with few high school or college graduates may not perceive college as an option and may not see any particular shame in dropping out. Taking academically talented poor and minority students who would be first-generation college attendees to spend time on college campuses, to see people like themselves and experience some of the pleasures of college life, is an important way to connect students psychologically to an attainable future.

Some effective programs address the defining element of poverty: lack of money. Many students drop out simply because they perceive the need to make money for themselves or for their families. In some communities, dropping out to get a job to help support the family is seen as a positive step, not one that alienates the student from his or her family or community. Therefore, some effective dropout prevention programs provide students with opportunities to earn money as long as they stay in high school. For example, the Coca-Cola Valued Youth Program pays students to tutor younger students, and Project GRAD provides opportunities for paid internships in local businesses as well as $1,000 college stipends.

All of the successful programs provide some form of academic assistance to help students perform well in their coursework. This is an obvious necessity; one of the key reasons students drop out is because of the frustration of failing classes and a feeling that their academic efforts will not pay off. Yet traditional remedial classes are not characteristic of the effective programs. Instead, academic assistance is provided in the form of small-group or individual tutorials, both on the content they are studying in class and on more generic study skills. The academic assistance in these programs is presented as a means of helping students keep up in high-track classes (as in AVID), to help them go to college (as in Upward Bound), or to improve their skills in tutoring others (as in the Valued Youth Program). All of these strategies capture the idea of academic assistance to meet a valued goal rather than low-status, low-track remedial programs in which there is often little expectation that assistance will lead to high-level performance.

Many of the successful programs attempt to give students status and recognition within the school for academic efforts. For example, the Coca-Cola Valued Youth Program gives at-risk students an opportunity to tutor younger children, a high status, responsible role. AVID essentially places promising at-risk students in top-track classes, with enough assistance to succeed there. Finally, most programs recognize the importance of families in the school success of their children, and provide activities to engage parents' efforts in support of their children's achievement and school completion.

There is not enough evidence from studies of dropout prevention and college attendance models to indicate which components of these comprehensive models is most effective or cost effective. Yet it is clear that these are effective approaches to increasing the graduate rates and college attendance of at-risk students. The existing successful approaches are intensive, comprehensive, and built around positive expectations for adolescents. They demonstrate that the problem of unacceptably high drop-out rates among students placed at risk is one we can solve. There is much more we need to learn about these programs, but we already know enough to take action on this critical problem.

Note

1. This chapter is adapted from Fashola and Slavin (in press a).

5

School District Strategies to Support School Change

◆

It is not enough to know what works and what is replicable. If schools are to reform themselves on a large scale, it is essential that they have the proactive support of their districts. Districts, intermediate units, state departments of education, and other agencies can play a key role in creating conditions in which school staffs can learn about, select, implement, and evaluate proven programs. In fact, this must be the primary goal of the entire reform process; any reform that stops short of the classroom door is unlikely to affect student achievement. The purpose of this chapter is to lay out a strategy that school districts can use to phase in effective methods on a broad scale and to ensure that they make a substantial difference in student performance. These same strategies could be used by states, intermediate units, regional service centers, or other agencies serving many individual districts. The strategy is intended to enable school staffs to learn about and select from among a range of proven programs known to make a difference in student performance, and then receive the support necessary to implement these programs with integrity, quality, and appropriate adaptations to school needs and resources. The strategy is similar in some ways to the process that New American Schools (NAS) is using in a few large cities (especially Memphis, Miami, and Cincinnati) and in the state of Maryland to introduce seven school designs developed under NAS funding (see Ross et al., 1997; Stringfield, Datnow, Herman, & Berkeley, 1997; and

Stringfield & Ross, 1997, for descriptions of the Memphis experience). The major elements of the strategy are described below.

Selecting an Initial Set of Effective Methods

The first step in a district process for introducing effective methods is to decide on an initial set of models to be offered to schools. The models should have several essential characteristics, as follows:

- Each should have been rigorously evaluated in comparison to traditional control groups on measures of achievement and found to be markedly more effective.
- Each should have available trainers, materials, assessments, and other supports to enable schools to readily replicate the model.
- Each should have a track record working in schools like those in the district, especially Title I schools.
- Each should be available and affordable to a large proportion of the district's schools.

Programs offered to schools might be of several types. One would be comprehensive school designs that address all of the essential requirements for schoolwide change: curriculum, instruction, assessment, provisions for students who are having difficulties keeping up, professional development, family support, and so on. Examples of these are included in Chapter 2. Alternatively, schools might assemble their own comprehensive designs from components that have been rigorously evaluated, such as those discussed in Chapter 3. For example, an elementary school might decide to implement the Direct Instruction reading program, Cognitively Guided Instruction in math, and Core Knowledge in science and social studies; use Reading Recovery as a tutoring model for at-risk first graders; adopt the Consistency Management program to improve classroom management and student behavior; and so on. In either case, program elements should be phased in over time, so that each can be effectively implemented before the next is introduced.

In addition to programs directly designed to enhance student achievement, programs or practices that accomplish other objectives might be identified. For example, effective approaches to induction of new teachers; selection and training of principals; multicultural education; improving intergroup relations; increasing parent involvement; or reducing violence, drug abuse, or early pregnancy might be identified and disseminated through a similar process. Secondary programs designed to reduce dropout and increase college attendance, such as those described in Chapter 4, would certainly be among those offered to middle or high schools.

Arranging Information and
Support for Program Adoption

Before introducing design options to schools, the district needs to figure out what is required to support each one. This involves assembling and synthesizing information on costs, requirements for released days for training, need for any waivers or direct assistance to schools, and so on. This information should be organized in a format that enables schools to make fair comparisons among alternative models and to help the district plan how to support each design. At the point when designs are offered to schools, district staffs should be clear on all of these practicalities, especially how the design costs will be paid for and what waivers from district or state policies will be sought or granted.

The school district needs to decide, and then communicate to schools, how the various programs fit into existing district or state initiatives. For example, schools might be told that their plan to adopt a given design may entirely constitute their Title I plan. Schools that are on a "watch list" of low-performing schools may be told that adopting and implementing a design will be considered an acceptable plan and may give the school an additional year's grace period before additional sanctions are applied. Schools may be assured that the designs will be aligned with district and state standards and assessments. Every effort should be made to communicate the idea that adoption of proven designs will not conflict with district or state policies and will in fact help accomplish them.

Selection of an Effective Methods Coordinator

As soon as possible, the district needs to designate a coordinator for the entire process of selecting and implementing proven programs. This should be a high-energy, enthusiastic, and well-organized person who is given full time to oversee the process of district design selection, awareness, effective methods fairs, follow-up, school selection of designs, and implementation. This person will be the key connection between the design teams and the school district. The importance of having a talented and energetic person in this role cannot be overstated.

Identifying Funding Sources

The district needs to identify sources of funding for the entire effective methods process. In general, it is important to rely primarily on funds schools already receive, such as Title I, state compensatory education, special education, and bilingual funds; professional development funds; textbook and materials funds; and so on. To assist with one-time start-up costs and to provide an incentive to schools to use existing funds to adopt proven reforms, schools might be offered grants to help them get going, on the order of $25,000 to $75,000 for 1 to 3 years. The recent congressional allocation of grants for start-up costs of adopting proven comprehensive reform designs is an obvious source of funds for this purpose. These grants should be given on the understanding that schools would align other funds and policies with the program and give a good-faith effort to implement the program with integrity and care. The idea is to provide enough money to help schools get going, but not so much that they become dependent on special funding (and drop the program when money runs out).

It is important to have a pool of money available for start-up funding in a moderate number of schools. In a large district, region, or state, any project involving only a few schools is likely to be lost or ignored. On the other hand, starting with too many schools risks disaster due to poor implementations or poor coordination. A plan that anticipates affecting a total of 10 to 25 schools implementing 3 to 5 different designs in the first year (in a district or region of 100 to 400 schools) may be about right, with a plan to add additional schools and designs in successive years.

Starting the School Awareness Process

As soon as an initial set of proven and promising designs is identified and the district has figured out how to support schools in adopting these designs, it is time to begin a process of making schools aware of the options they have, leading up to an opportunity for school staffs to make an informed choice. A centerpiece of this awareness process is the effective methods fair, described below, but it is a mistake to have the effective methods fair take place before a great deal of groundwork has been laid.

Districts may wish to restrict in advance the pool of schools eligible to choose designs in a given year. For example, they might focus initial efforts on Title I schoolwide projects, which are likely to have the funding and the flexibility to adopt programs. They might focus on schools on a list of underperforming schools. They might initially limit the process to elementary schools, which typically have a broader range of design options available. They might decide to exclude schools currently undergoing changes in principals. However, it is important not to restrict the pool too much, which could have the effect of ensuring that certain schools will be selected (and that they therefore need not promise much to get the money). The ideal circumstance is one in which there are two or three times (or more) as many eligible schools as there are available spots, so that the schools need to convince the district and design teams that they are ready and willing to adopt the design, not the other way around.

The awareness process might start with a principal's meeting, at which the district superintendent and other central office staff explain the overall plan and distribute awareness materials on the selected designs. The following are key ideas to be communicated at this meeting and in other contexts:

- The district is strongly committed to the effective methods process.
- Schools will be strongly encouraged and supported in adopting proven designs.

- Decisions about which (if any) designs are to be implemented will be made by school staffs by secret ballot; designs will not be imposed on schools by the central office or by principals. Schools will not be pressured to take on any design but may decide to wait for opportunities in later years.
- Awareness of alternative designs among school staff, parents, and community members is essential. Schools need to make informed choices.
- Most funding for design adoption will come from the schools' own resources, such as Title I. Any additional funds being made available are for start-up, not long-term program implementation.
- There are a limited number of slots available in the first year. To be included in the first wave, schools need to show widespread, informed enthusiasm for a design; a well-worked-out plan of implementation; and a plan to focus existing resources around the design's requirements.

Principals interested in going on to the next step might be given awareness materials for their staff and parent groups, and copies of videos on each design. They might be asked to show the videos and distribute materials over the course of several staff and parent meetings, if time allows. Principals should be encouraged to let their staffs explore all options, not focus in immediately on one.

Effective Methods Fair

An effective methods fair is an event to which school teams are invited to hear directly from representatives of various designs and have opportunities to more fully examine materials, view videos, and ask questions about several alternatives. The effective methods fair should have a certain level of hoopla and hype to energize participants and let them know how important this whole process is to the district, but it should also be packed with practical, down-to-earth information.

School teams invited to an effective methods fair should include the principal, several teachers, and one or more activist parents. The design of the fair should allow participants to learn about three to four different designs in repeated sessions.

It is important to try to make sure that all fair participants know something about the designs and about the district's arrangements to facilitate adoption of several designs before the fair takes place. The fair should help participants move toward final decisions, not just start an awareness process.

The districts should schedule an effective methods fair about 1 month after the first meeting with principals. The effective methods fair should take place no later than February, if possible, to allow enough time for schools to make an informed choice and then do the planning necessary for a successful implementation in September. A key date to watch is the date when Title I plans are due (usually March); it is critical to have Title I plans reflect the requirements of the designs. The awareness schedule should enable schools to write their Title I plans after having made their choice of designs.

Post-Fair Follow-Up and Selection of Designs

Shortly after the fair, schools should be contacted about their interest in pursuing particular designs. Visits to schools by design team staff may be scheduled, and visits of delegations from the schools to schools implementing these designs should also be arranged. Within 3 to 4 weeks after the effective methods fair, schools should make their selections. In our own programs, Success for All and Roots and Wings, we require a vote by at least 80% of all certified staff. Most other designs have a similar requirement, or should have one.

Implementation Planning

After schools have made their decisions, they will need to work with design team representatives to plan training, materials ordering, staffing, and funding of the design. The district's effective methods coordinator should be involved in these discussions to help ensure that district policies support the implementation requirements of each design and to help resolve any problems that come up.

Evaluation

From the outset, the district needs to plan an evaluation of each design, both in terms of quality of implementation and outcome. Design teams might be asked for implementation benchmarks to enable schools and districts to know what is supposed to be implemented by when, and then school leaders and design team staff can report on a regular basis how each school is progressing toward full implementation. In terms of student outcomes, the district might collect data on the current spring cohort of students (before the program begins) and then repeat the same measurement each following spring to allow for assessments of growth. Alternatively, or in addition, matched control schools could be identified for each participating school, and student outcome assessments could then be compared over a period of years. The emphasis of the evaluation should not just be on whether each design works, but also on what it takes to ensure the effectiveness of each. For example, if some schools implementing a given design produce marvelous outcomes and some do not, the replicable characteristics of the more effective implementations could be studied to decide how the design might be modified to be as effective as that being implemented in the schools with better outcomes.

However, there are sure to be designs that just don't work out in individual schools or across the board, and schools need to be free to drop out of designs that are not working for them.

Over a period of years, as additional designs are introduced and then evaluated in a variety of districts, the districts themselves as well as the nation as a whole will gain increasing sophistication about what kinds of school change designs work in what situations, and learn how to ensure the success of schoolwide change designs.

Expansion Over Time

The district should have a long-term plan to gradually expand the number of schools adopting proven designs, as well as to build its own capacity to support quality implementations. Each year, schools might be offered a set of design options that incorporates additional designs as well as new knowledge about how to make sure the designs are effectively implemented. As the number of schools implementing any particular design grows, it makes sense for the district to build its own training and follow-up capacity for the design.

The effective methods process described in this chapter is one means of introducing proven, replicable schoolwide reform models to many schools in large districts, regions, or states. The cornerstone of the process is ensuring school staffs a free choice among appealing alternatives known, if well implemented, to significantly accelerate student achievement. This process, modeled on the methods New American Schools have used to introduce new designs to more than 750 schools in 10 large jurisdictions, respects the rights of teachers and principals to choose their own paths to reform but avoids requiring every school to reinvent the wheel. America's children need and deserve the best materials and teaching methods we know how to provide them. We need to learn how to transform teachers' daily practices, to use state-of-the-art methods tied to demanding standards of performance. We need to learn how to do this on a very large scale, especially in schools serving many children placed at risk. This chapter provides one model for how to accomplish this critical task.

Conclusion: Show Me the Evidence!

The research and experience presented in this book supports two seemingly inconsistent conclusions. First, there is a broad range of replicable programs from which elementary and secondary schools can choose to meet the needs of their students. Most of these are backed up by networks of trainers and experienced users, materials, manuals, videos, and other supports, and some have convincing evidence of effectiveness. Anyone who believes that the often dismal performance of many low-income and minority students is inevitable must confront the data from these programs. Anyone who believes that every school must reinvent its own path to reform must confront the evidence of replicability presented by so many programs. Some of the programs (such as Accelerated Schools, the School Development Project, and many of the New American Schools designs) are designed to help schools develop their own approaches, but this is not the same as asking schools without the support of these experienced and skillful networks to reinvent their practices. Of course, there is no "magic bullet"; quality of implementation must be a concern with any program, no matter how effective it has been elsewhere. However, although every program requires adaptation to the circumstances, needs, and resources of every school, it would be foolish for schools to ignore the rich and varied set of alternatives available to them to enhance the learning of their students.

Yet it is also important to note the enormous gaps in our knowledge base. It is sobering to find so few studies of effective and replicable practices, especially schoolwide models. Clearly, there is a need for far more research and development specifically designed to produce and evaluate effective and replicable models for schools to use (see Slavin, 1997).

Although the number of proven programs and the quality of evidence for student achievement is not always what we'd wish for, there are most certainly many more effective programs in existence than those we have identified. Programs were seldom rejected from this review because we had evidence that they were not effective; instead, most simply lacked even rudimentary evidence to establish their effectiveness. Better evaluations of promising, attractive programs for students placed at risk would probably find many more effective and replicable models to add to our list.

The message of this review is one of hope and urgency. Schools can do a much better job of educating all students, especially low-income and minority students, using methods and materials that are readily available. There are approaches that are effective and appropriate for a wide variety of objectives. The existence of these approaches demonstrates that the low achievement of so many students placed at risk is not inevitable. We need not wait for social or political transformation to dramatically improve educational outcomes for students placed at risk of school failure. There is more we would want to know about existing programs, and there are many areas in which more and better programs are desperately needed, yet if we used what we do know now about programs that work we could make an enormous difference in the lives of all of our children.

Resource:
Contacts for Information and
Training on Programs Reviewed

◆

Accelerated Schools
Claudette Spriggs
National Center for the Accelerated Schools Project
Stanford University
CERAS 109
Stanford, CA 94305-3084
(415) 725-7158 or (415) 725-1676

ALAS
Katherine A. Larson & Russel W. Rumberger
University of California, Santa Barbara
Graduate School of Education
Phelps Hall
Santa Barbara, CA 93106

ATLAS Communities
Linda Gerstle
Education Development Center
55 Chapel St.
Newton, MA 02160
(617) 969-7100 ext. 2470
FAX (617) 969-3440

Audrey Cohen College
Janith Jordan
345 Hudson St.
New York, NY 10014
(212) 989-2002 ext. 223
FAX (212) 675-0603

AVID
Mary Catherine Swanson
Director, AVID program
San Diego County Office of Education
6401 Linda Vista Road
San Diego, CA 92111-7399
(619) 292-3500

Bilingual Cooperative Integrated Reading and Composition (BCIRC)
Margarita Calderón
1816 Larry Hinson
El Paso, TX 79936
(915) 595-5971

Coalition of Essential Schools
Theodore Sizer, Chairman
Brown University
Box 1969
Providence, RI 02912
(401) 863-3384

Coca-Cola Valued Youth Project
Linda Cantu, Project Director
Intercultural Development Research Association
Coca-Cola Valued Youth Program
5835 Callaghan, Suite 350
San Antonio, TX 78228-1190
(210) 684-8180
(210) 684-5389

Cognitively Guided Instruction (CGI)
Elizabeth Fennema or Thomas Carpenter
University of Wisconsin—Madison
Wisconsin Center for Education Research
1025 West Johnson Street
Madison, WI 53706
(608) 263-4265

Complex Instruction/Finding Out/Descubrimiento
Elizabeth G. Cohen
Stanford University, School of Education
Stanford, CA 94305
(415) 723-4661

Comprehensive School Mathematics Program (CSMP)
Clare Heidema, Director, CSMP
2550 South Parker Road, Suite 500
Aurora, CO 80014
(303) 337-0990; Voice mail (303) 743-5520
FAX (303) 337-3005

Co-NECT Schools
Dr. John Richards
Educational Technologies
Bolt, Beranek and Newman
150 Cambridge Park Dr.
Cambridge, MA 02138
(617) 873-3081
FAX (617) 873-3776

Consistency Management and Cooperative Discipline (CMCD)
H. Jerome Freiberg
University of Houston
College of Education
Houston, TX 77204-5872
(713) 743-8663

Cooperative Integrated Reading and Composition (CIRC)
Anna Marie Farnish
Center for Social Organization of Schools
The Johns Hopkins University
3505 North Charles Street
Baltimore, MD 21218
(410) 516-8857
FAX (410) 516-8890

Core Knowledge
E. D. Hirsch
Core Knowledge Foundation
2012-B Morton Dr.
Charlottesville, VA 22903
(804) 977-7550

Direct Instruction/DISTAR
Association for Direct Instruction
805 Lincoln
Eugene, OR 97401
(541) 485-1293

Early Intervention for School Success
Dean Hiser
200 Calmus Drive
P.O. Box 9050
Costa Mesa CA 92628-9050
(714) 900-4125

Edison Project
Deborah Doorack
521 5th Ave., 16th Fl.
New York, NY 10175
(212) 309-1600

Exemplary Center for Reading Instruction (ECRI)
Ethna R. Reid
Reid Foundation, 3310 South 2700 East
Salt Lake City, UT 84109
(801) 486-5083 or (801) 278-2334
FAX (801) 485-0561

Expeditionary Learning/Outward Bound
Margaret M. Campbell
122 Mount Auburn St.
Cambridge, MA 02138
(617) 576-1260
FAX (617) 576-1340

Goldenberg and Sullivan
Claude Goldenberg
Dept. of Teacher Education
CSU Long Beach
1250 Bellflower Blvd.
Long Beach, CA 90840
(310) 985-5733
FAX (310) 985-1543

GRAD
J. L. Ketelsen
P.O. Box 2511
Houston, TX 77001
(713) 757-3563

High/Scope Educational Research Foundation (Perry Preschool)
A. C. Shouse, Director, Development and Services
600 North River Street
Ypsilanti, MI 48198
(313) 485-2000
FAX (313) 485-0704

Jigsaw
Spencer Kagan
Resources for Teachers
27134 A Paseo Espada #202
San Juan, Capistrano, CA 92675
(800) WEE-COOP

Learning Together
Roger T. Johnson and David W. Johnson
The Cooperative Learning Center
60 Peik Hall, University of Minnesota
Minneapolis, MN 55455
(612) 624-7031

Maneuvers With Mathematics (MWM)
David A. Page or Kathryn B. Chval
The University of Illinois at Chicago
851 Morgan Street, (m/c 249) SEO 1309
Chicago, IL 60607-7045
(312) 996-8708

Modern Red Schoolhouse
Sally B. Kilgore
Hudson Institute
5395 Emerson Way
Indianapolis, IN 46226
(317) 545-1000
FAX (317) 545-1384

Multi-Cultural Reading and Thinking (McRAT)
Janita Hoskyn, National Consultant, McRAT Program
1019 Ronwood Drive
Little Rock, AR 72227
(501) 225-5809
FAX (501) 455-4137

National Alliance for Restructuring Education
Marc S. Tucker
700 11th Street, NW
Suite 750
Washington, DC 20001
(202) 783-3668
FAX (202) 783-3672

Paideia
Terry Roberts
National Paideia Center
School of Education
CB 8045
UNC-CH
Chapel Hill, NC 27599-8045
(919) 962-7379
FAX (919) 962-7381

Profile Approach to Writing
Jane B. Hughey, Dixie Copeland
1701 Southwest Parkway, Suite 102
College Station, TX 77840
(409) 764-9765 Phone or FAX

Project SEED (Berkeley, California)
Helen Smiler, National Projects Coordinator
2530 San Pablo Avenue, Suite K
Berkeley, CA 94702
(510) 644-3422
FAX (510) 644-0566

Project SEED (Dallas, Texas)
Hamid Ebrahimi, National Director
3414 Oak Grove Avenue
Dallas, Texas 75204
(214) 954-0507

Reading Recovery/Descubriendo La Lectura
Carol A. Lyons, Gay Su Pinnell, or Diane E. DeFord
Reading Recovery Program
The Ohio State University, 200 Ramseyer Hall
29 West Woodruff Avenue
Columbus, OH 42310
(614) 292-7807
FAX (614) 688-3646

Reciprocal Teaching
Anne Marie Palincsar
University of Michigan, Ann Arbor
4204c SEB
610 E University
Ann Arbor, MI 48109

School Development Program (SDP)
Ed Joyner
Child Study Center
School Development Program
230 South Frontage Road
P.O. Box 20790
New Haven, Connecticut 06520-7900
(203) 785-2548
FAX (203) 785-3359

SCORE
Sharon Marshall Johnson
Orange County Department of Education
200 Kalmus Drive
Post Office Box 9050
Costa Mesa, CA 92628-9050
(714) 966-4394 or (714) 966-4388
FAX (714) 662-3148

Skills Reinforcement Project (SRP)
Elizabeth Jones Stork, Director, IAAY Western Region, and Deputy
    Director, CAA
The Johns Hopkins University, Western Regional Office
206 North Jackson Street, Suite 304
Glendale, CA 91206
(818) 500-9034
FAX (818) 500-9058

**Student Teams–Achievement Divisions and Teams-Games-
Tournaments**
Anna Marie Farnish
Center for Social Organization of Schools
The Johns Hopkins University
3505 North Charles Street
Baltimore, MD 21218
(410) 516-8857
FAX (410) 516-8890

Success for All/Roots and Wings
Robert E. Slavin
Center for Social Organization of Schools
The Johns Hopkins University
3505 North Charles Street
Baltimore, MD 21218
(800) 548-4998
FAX (410) 516-8890

Upward Bound
David Goodwin
U.S. Department of Education
600 C Independence Avenue SW
Washington, DC 20202
(202) 401-0182

References

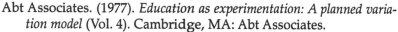

Abt Associates. (1977). *Education as experimentation: A planned variation model* (Vol. 4). Cambridge, MA: Abt Associates.

Adams, G. L., & Engelmann, S. (1996). *Research on Direct Instruction: 25 years beyond DISTAR*. Seattle, WA: Educational Achievement Systems.

Adler, M. J. (1982). *The Paideia proposal: An educational manifesto.* New York: Macmillan.

Arkansas Department of Education (1992). *Multicultural Reading and Thinking (McRat).* Proposal submitted to the Program Effectiveness Panel of the National Diffusion Network. Washington, DC: U.S. Department of Education.

Aronson, E., Blaney, N., Stephan, C., Sikes, J., & Snapp, M. (1978). *The Jigsaw classroom.* Beverly Hills, CA: Sage.

Baenen, N., Bernholc, A., Dulaney, C., Banks, K., Willoughby, M. (1995). *Evaluation report: WCPSS Reading Recovery 1990-1994.* Raleigh, NC: Wake County Public Schools.

Becker, B. J., & Hedges, L. V. (1992). *A review of the literature on the effectiveness of Comer's School Development Program.* Unpublished manuscript, Michigan State University.

Becker, W. C., & Gersten, R. (1982). A follow-up of Follow Through: The later effects of the Direct Instruction model on children in fifth and sixth grades. *American Educational Research Journal, 19* (1), 75-92.

Bereiter, C., & Engelmann, S. (1966). *Teaching disadvantaged children in the preschool.* Englewood Cliffs, NJ.: Prentice Hall.

Bodilly, S. J. (1996). *Lessons from the New American Schools Development Corporation's Development Phase.* Washington, DC: RAND.

Burkheimer, G. J., Levinsohn, J. R., Koo, J. P., & French, A. M. (1976). *Final report: A study of the National Upward Bound and Talent Search Programs.* Research Triangle Park, Durham, N.C.: Research Triangle Institute, Center for Educational Research and Evaluation.

Burkheimer, G. J., Riccobono, J., & Wisenbaker, J. (1979). *Final report: Evaluation study of the Upward Bound Program—A second follow-up.* Durham, N.C.: Research Triangle Institute, Center for Educational Research and Evaluation.

Calderón, M., Hertz-Lazarowitz, & Slavin, R. E. (in press). Effects of Bilingual Cooperative Integrated Reading and Composition on students transitioning from Spanish to English reading. *Elementary School Journal.*

Calderón, M., Tinajero, J., & Hertz-Lazarowitz, R. (1992). Adapting CIRC to meet the needs of bilingual students. *Journal of Educational Issues of Linguistic Minority Students, 10,* 79-106.

Campbell, M., Farrell, G., Kamii, M., Lam, D., Rugen, L., & Udall, D. (1996). The expeditionary learning Outward Bound design. In S. Stringfield, S. Ross, & L. Smith (Eds.), *Bold plans for school restructuring: The New American Schools Development Corporation Designs.* Mahwah, NJ: Erlbaum.

Cardenas, J. A., Montecel, M. R., Supik, J. D., & Harris, R. J. (1992). The Coca-Cola Valued Youth Program: Dropout prevention strategies for at-risk students. *Texas Researcher, 3,* 111-130.

Carey, D. A., Fennema, E., Carpenter, T. P., & Franke, M. L. (1993). Equity and mathematics education. In W. Secada, E. Fennema, & L. Byrd (Eds.), *New directions in equity for mathematics education.* New York: Teachers College Press.

Carpenter, T. P., Fennema, E., Peterson, P. L., Chiang, C. P., Loef, M. (1989). Using knowledge of children's mathematics thinking in classroom teaching: An experimental study. *American Educational Research Journal, 26*(4), 499-531.

Center, Y., Wheldall, K., Freeman, L., Outhred, L., & McNaught, M. (1995). An evaluation of Reading Recovery. *Reading Research Quarterly, 30,* 240-261.

Clay, M. M. (1985). *The early detection of reading difficulties.* Exeter, NH: Heinemann.

Coca-Cola Valued Youth Program. (1991). Proposal submitted to the Program Effectiveness Panel of the U.S. Department of Education. Washington, DC: U.S. Department of Education.

Cohen, A., & Jordan, J. (1996). The Audrey Cohen College System of Education: Purpose-centered education. In S. Stringfield, S. Ross, & L. Smith (Eds.), *Bold plans for school restructuring: The New American Schools Development Corporation Designs.* Mahwah, NJ: Erlbaum.

Cohen, E. G. (1984). Talking and working together: Status, interaction, and learning. In P. Peterson, L. C. Wilkinson, & M. Hallinan (Eds.), *Instructional groups in the classroom* (pp. 171-188). Orlando, FL: Academic Press,

Cohen, E. G. (1994a). *Designing groupwork: Strategies for the heterogeneous classroom* (2nd ed.). New York: Teachers College Press.

Cohen, E. G. (1994b). Restructuring the classroom: Conditions for productive small groups. *Review of Educational Research, 64*(1), 1-35.

Cohen, E. G., & Intili, J. K. (1981). *Interdependence and management in bilingual classrooms.* Unpublished technical report, Stanford University.

Cohen, E. G., Lotan, R., & Leechor, C. (1989). Can classrooms learn? *Sociology of Education, 62,* 75-94.

Cohen, P. A., Kulik, J. A., & Kulik, C.L.C. (1982). Educational outcomes of tutoring: A meta-analysis of findings. *American Educational Research Journal, 19,* 237-248.

Comer, J. (1980). *School power.* New York: Free Press.

Comer, J. (1988). Educating poor minority children. *Scientific American, 259,* 42-48.

Comer, J., Gardner, H., Sizer, T., & Whitla, J. (1996). ATLAS Communities: Authentic teaching, learning for all students. In S. Stringfield, S. Ross, & L. Smith (Eds.), *Bold plans for school restructuring: The New American Schools Development Corporation Designs.* Mahwah, NJ: Erlbaum.

Comer, J. P., Haynes, N. M., Joyner, E. T., & Ben-Avie, M. (1996). *Rallying the whole village: The Comer process for reforming education.* New York: Teachers College Press.

Comprehensive School Mathematics Program. (1995). *Comprehensive School Mathematics Program: Submission to the Program Effectiveness Panel.* Washington, DC: U.S. Department of Education.

Core Knowledge Foundation. (1995). *Core knowledge sequence.* Charlottesville, VA: Author.

DeAvila, E. A., & Duncan, S. E. (1980). *Finding out/Descubrimiento.* Corte Madera, CA: Linguametrics Group.

DeFord, Pinnell, G. S., Lyons, C., & Young, P. (1988). *Reading Recovery: Volume IX, report on the follow-up studies.* Columbus, OH: Ohio State University.

Dianda, M., & Flaherty, J. (1995, April). *Effects of Success for All on the reading achievement of first graders in California bilingual programs.* Paper presented at the annual meeting of the American Educational Research Association, San Francisco.

Early intervention for school success. (1986). Annual report to the California State Legislature. Sacramento: California State Department of Education.

Early Intervention for School Success. (1995). Proposal submitted to the Program Effectiveness Panel of the National Diffusion Network. Washington, DC: U.S. Department of Education.

Edgar, E., & Johnson, E. (1995). Belief Academy: Project evaluation, 1990-1995. In U.S. Department of Education, *Staying in school: The ABC dropout prevention and intervention series.* Washington, DC: Author.

Edison Project. (1996). *Edison Project partnership schools show promising academic gains one year after opening.* New York: Author.

Educational Testing Service. (1995). *Dreams deferred: High school dropouts in the United States.* Princeton, NJ: Author.

Ekstrom, R. B., Goertz, M. E., Pollack, J. M., & Rock, D. A. (1986). Who drops out of high school and why? *Teacher's College Record, 87,* 356-373.

Elmore, R. F. (1996). Getting to scale with good educational practice. *Harvard Educational Review, 66,* 1-26.

Epstein, J. L., Salinas, K. C., & Jackson, V. E. (1995). *TIPS: Teachers involve parents in schoolwork* (Rev. ed.). Baltimore, MD: Johns Hopkins University, Center on Families, Communities, Schools, and Children's Learning.

Escamilla, K. (1994). Descubriendo La Lectura: An early intervention literacy program in Spanish. *Literacy, Teaching, and Learning, 1*(1), 57-70.

Fashola, O. S., & Slavin, R. E. (1997). Promising programs for elementary and middle schools: Evidence of effectiveness and replicability. *Journal of Education for Students Placed at Risk, 2*(3), 251-307.

Fashola, O. S., & Slavin, R. E. (in press a). Effective dropout prevention and college attendance programs for students placed at risk. *Journal of Education for Students Placed at Risk.*

Fashola, O. S., & Slavin, R. E. (in press b). Schoowide reform models: What works? *Phi Delta Kappan.*

Finn, J. D. (1989). Withdrawing from school. *Review of Educational Research, 59,* 117-142.

Freiberg, H. J. (1996). *Consistency management and cooperative discipline: A sample design.* Houston, TX: University of Houston.

Freiberg, H. J., & Huang, S. (1994). *Final report study 2.4: The longitudinal study of the life cycle of improving schools (year ending October 31, 1993).* Philadelphia: National Center on Education in the Inner Cities.

Freiberg, H. J., Prokosch, N., & Treister, E. S. (1990). Turning around five at-risk elementary schools. *School Effectiveness and School Improvement 1*(1), 5-25.

Freiberg, H. J., Stein, T. A., & Huang, S. (1995). Effects of a classroom management intervention on student achievement in inner-city elementary schools. *Educational Research and Evaluation, 1* (1), 36-66.

Glass, G. V., McGaw, B., & Smith, M. L. (1981). *Meta-analysis in social research.* Beverly Hills, CA: Sage.

Goertz, M. E., Floden, R. E., & O'Day, J. (1996). *Studies of education reform: Systematic reform.* Philadelphia: University of Pennsylvania, Consortium for Policy Research in Education.

Goldberg, B., & Richards, J. (1996). Co-NECT Schools. In S. Stringfield, S. Ross, & L. Smith (Eds.), *Bold plans for school restructuring: The New American Schools Development Corporation Designs.* Mahwah, NJ: Erlbaum.

Gonzales, A. (1981). *An approach to interdependent/cooperative bilingual education measures related to social motives.* Fresno: California State University at Fresno.

Hartfiel, V. F., Hughey, J. B., Wormuth, D. R., & Jacobs, H. C. (1985). *Learning ESL composition.* Rowley, MA: Newberry House.

Haynes, N. M. (1991). *Summary of School Development Program documentation and research.* New Haven, CT: Yale Child Study Center.

Haynes, N. M. (Ed.). (1994). *School Development Program research monograph.* New Haven, CT: Yale Child Study Center.

Hayward, B. J., & Tallmadge, G. K. (1995). *Strategies for keeping kids in school: Evaluation of dropout prevention and reentry projects in vocational education.* Washington, DC: U.S. Department of Education.

Herman, R., & Stringfield, S. (1995, April). *Ten promising programs for educating disadvantaged students: Evidence of impact.* Paper presented at the annual meeting of the American Educational Research Association, San Francisco.

Herman, R., & Stringfield, S. (1997). *Ten promising programs for educating disadvantaged students: Evidence of impact.* Arlington, VA: Educational Research Service.

Hertz-Lazarowitz, R., Lerner, M., Schaedel, B., Walk, A., & Sarid, M. (1996). Story-related writing: An evaluation of CIRC in Israel. *Helkat-Lashon (Journal of Linguistic Education, 22,* 85-113, in Hebrew).

Hillocks, G. (1984). What works in teaching composition: A meta-analysis of experimental treatment studies. *American Journal of Education, 93,* 133-170.

Hirsch, E. D. (1987). *Cultural literacy: What every American needs to know.* New York: Random House.

Hirsch, E. D. (1991a). *What your first grader needs to know.* New York: Doubleday.

Hirsch, E. D. (1991b). *What your second grader needs to know.* New York: Doubleday.

Hirsch, E. D. (1992a). *What your third grader needs to know.* New York: Doubleday.

Hirsch, E. D. (1992b). *What your fourth grader needs to know.* New York: Doubleday.

Hirsch, E. D. (1993a). The core knowledge curriculum: What's behind its success? *Educational Leadership, 50*(8), 23-30.

Hirsch, E. D. (1993b). *What your fifth grader needs to know.* New York: Doubleday.

Hirsch, E. D. (1993c). *What your sixth grader needs to know.* New York: Doubleday.

Hollins, E. R., Smiler, H., & Spencer, K. (1994). Benchmarks in meeting the challenges of effective schooling for African American youngsters. In E. R. Hollins, J. E. King, & W. C. Hayman (Eds.), *Teaching diverse populations: Formulating a knowledge base.* Albany: State University of New York Press.

Hopfenberg, W. S., & Levin, H. M. (1993). *The Accelerated Schools resource guide.* San Francisco: Jossey-Bass.

Huck, C. S., & Pinnell, G. S. (1986). *The Reading Recovery project in Columbus, Ohio: Pilot year, 1984-85.* Columbus: Ohio State University.

Hughey, J. B., & Hartfiel, V. F. (1979). *Profile approach to writing.* College Station, TX: Profile Writing Program Incorporated.

Hughey, J. B., Wormuth, D. R., Hartfiel, V. F., & Jacobs, H. L. (1985). *Teaching ESL composition: Principles and techniques.* Rowley, MA: Newberry House.

Jacobs, H. L., Zinkgraf, S. A., Wormuth, D. R., Hartfiel, V. F., & Hughey, J. B. (1981). *Testing ESL Composition: A practical approach.* Rowley, MA: Newberry House.

Johnson, D. W., & Johnson, R. T. (1994). *Learning together and alone: Cooperative, competitive, and individualistic learning* (4th ed.). Boston: Allyn & Bacon.

Johnson, S. G. (1983). *A survey of SCORE for college.* Unpublished master's thesis. California State University, Fullerton.

Johntz, W. F. (1966, January). Mathematics and the culturally disadvantaged. *Bulletin of the California Mathematics Council.*

Johntz, W. F. (1975). *Project SEED and its implications for mathematics education internationally. The teaching of algebra at the pre-college level.* St. Louis, MO: CEMREL.

Kagan, S. (1995). *Cooperative learning.* Boston: Charlesbridge.

Karweit, N. L. (1989). Effective preschool programs for students at risk. In Slavin, R. E., Karweit, N. L., & Madden, N. A. (Eds.), *Effective programs for students at risk.* Boston: Allyn & Bacon.

Karweit, N. L. (1994). Can preschool alone prevent early reading failure? In R. E. Slavin, N. L. Karweit, & B. A. Wasik (Eds.). *Preventing early school failure.* Boston: Allyn & Bacon.

Kelly, P. R., Gomez-Valdez, C., Klein, A. F., & Neal, J. C. (1995, April). *Progress of first and second language learners in an early intervention program.* Paper presented at the annual meeting of the American Educational Research Association, San Francisco.

Ketelsen, J. L. (1994). *Jefferson Davis Feeder School Project.* Houston, TX: Tenneco Corporation, Project GRAD.

Kilgore, S. Doyle, D., & Linkowsky, L. (1996). The modern red schoolhouse. In S. Stringfield, S. Ross, & L. Smith (Eds.), *Bold plans for school restructuring: The New American Schools Development Corporation Designs.* Mahwah, NJ: Erlbaum.

Knight, S. L., & Stallings, J. A. (1995). The implementation of the Accelerated School model in an urban elementary school. In R. L. Allington & S. A. Walmsley (Eds.), *No quick fix: Rethinking literacy programs in America's elementary schools* (pp. 236-252). New York: Teachers College Press.

Larson, K., & Rumberger, R. (1995). Doubling school success in highest-risk Latino youth: Results from a middle school intervention study. In R. F. Macias & R. Garcia Ramos (Eds.), *Changing schools for changing students.* Santa Barbara: University of California at Santa Barbara.

Levin, H. M. (1987). Accelerated schools for disadvantaged students. *Educational Leadership, 44*(6), 19-21.

Long, U. M. (1993). UIC-MWMI: A model middle grades mathematics reform project. *The Mathematics Teacher 86*(3), pp. 121-126.

Lucker, B., Rosenfield, D., Sikes, J., & Aronson, E. (1976). Performance in the independent classroom: A field study. *American Educational Research Journal, 13,* 115-123.

Lynch, S., & Mills, C. J. (1990). The Skills Reinforcement Project: An academic program for high potential minority youth. *Journal for the Education of the Gifted, 13*(4), 364-379.

Madden, N. A., Slavin, R. E., Farnish, A. M., Livingston, M. A., Calderón, M., & Stevens, R. J. (1996). *Reading Wings: Teacher's manual*. Baltimore: Johns Hopkins University, Center for Research on the Education of Students Placed at Risk.

Madden, N. A., Slavin, R. E., & Simons, K. (1997). *MathWings: Early indicators of effectiveness*. Baltimore: Johns Hopkins University, Center for Research on the Education of Students Placed at Risk.

Maneuvers with mathematics. (1991). Proposal submitted to the Program Effectiveness Panel of the National Diffusion Network. Washington, DC: U.S. Department of Education.

Maneuvers with mathematics. (1995). Proposal submitted to the Program Effectiveness Panel of the National Diffusion Network. Washington, DC: U.S. Department of Education.

Marshall, M. (1996). *Core Knowledge sequence credited in test score boosts*. Charlottesville, VA: Core Knowledge Foundation.

Mattingly, R. M., & Van Sickle, R. L. (1991). Cooperative learning and achievement in social studies: Jigsaw II. *Social Education, 55*(6), 392-395.

McCarthy, J., & Still, S. (1993). Hollibrook Accelerated Elementary School. In J. Murphy & P. Hallinger (Eds.), *Restructuring schooling: Learning from ongoing efforts* (pp. 63-83). Newbury Park, CA: Corwin.

McKey, R., Condelli, L., Ganson, H., Barrett, B., McConkey, C., & Plantz, M. (1985). *The impact of Head Start on children, families, and communities* (DHHS Publication No. [OHDS] 85-31193). Washington, DC: U.S. Government Printing Office.

McLaughlin, M. W. (1990). The Rand change agent study revisited: Macro perspectives and micro realities. *Educational Researcher, 19*(9), 11-16.

Mehan, H., Datnow, A., Bratton, E., Tellez, C., Friedlander, D., & Ngo, T. (1992). *Untracking and college enrollment* (Research Report: 4). Santa Cruz, CA: National Center for Research on Cultural Diversity and Second Language Learning, University of California, Santa Cruz.

Mehan, H., Villanueva, I., Hubbard, L., & Lintz, A. (1996). *Constructing school success: The consequences of untracking low-achieving students*. New York: Cambridge University Press.

Meyer, L. A. (1984). Long-term academic effects of the Direct Instruction Project follow-through. *Elementary School Journal, 84*, 380-394.

Mills, C. J. (1992). Reflections on recognition and development of academic talent in educationally disadvantaged students. *Exceptionality, 3,* 189-192.

Mills, C. J., Stork, E. J., & Krug, K. (1992). Recognition and development of academic talent in educationally disadvantaged students. *Exceptionality, 3,* 165-180.

Muncey, D. E., & McQuillan, P. J. (1996). *Reform and resistance in schools and classrooms: An ethnographic view of the Coaliton of Essential Schools.* New Haven, CT: Yale University Press.

National Center for Education Statistics. (1993). *Dropout rates in the U.S.* Washington, DC: U.S. Department of Education.

National Center for Education Statistics. (1995). *The educational progress of Hispanic students.* Washington, DC: U.S. Department of Education.

National Center for Education Statistics. (1996). *Dropout rates in the United States: 1994.* Washington, DC: U.S. Department of Education.

National Commission on Excellence in Education. (1983). *A nation at risk.* Washington, DC: Author.

National Diffusion Network. (1995). *Educational programs that work: The catalogue of the National Diffusion Network* (21st ed.). Longmont, CO: Sopris West.

Newmann, F. M., King, M. B., & Rigdon, M. (1997). Accountability and school performance: Implications from restructuring schools. *Harvard Educational Review, 67,* 41-74.

Nunnery, J., Ross, S., Smith, L., Slavin, R., Hunter, P., & Stubbs, J. (1996, April). *An assessment of Success for All program component configuration effects on the reading achievement of at-risk first grade students.* Paper presented at the annual meeting of the American Educational Research Association, New York.

Opuni, K. B. (1995). *Project GRAD: Program evaluation report.* Houston, TX: Houston Independent School District.

Page, D. A. (1989). *The University of Illinois Arithmetic Project: Teacher education materials.* Newton, MA: Education Development Center.

Palincsar, A. S., & Brown, A. L. (1984). Reciprocal teaching of comprehension fostering and comprehension-monitoring activities. *Cognition and Instruction, 2,* 117-175.

Pfannenstiel, J., Lambson, T., & Yarnell, V. (1991). *Second wave study of the Parents as Teachers Program (final report).* St. Louis: Missouri Department of Elementary and Secondary Education and Parents as Teachers National Center.

Phillips, H., & Ebrahimi, H. (1993). Equation for success: Project SEED. In G. Cuevas & M. Driscoll (Eds.), *Reaching all students with mathematics*. Reston, VA: National Council of Teachers of Mathematics.

Pinnell, G. S. (1988, April). *Sustained effects of a strategy-centered early intervention program in reading*. Paper presented at the annual convention of the American Educational Research Association, New Orleans.

Pinnell, G. S. (1989). Reading Recovery: Helping at-risk children learn to read. *Elementary School Journal, 90,* 161-182.

Pinnell, G. S., DeFord, D. E., & Lyons, C. A. (1988). *Reading Recovery: Early intervention for at-risk first graders*. Arlington, VA: Education Research Service.

Pinnell, G. S., Lyons, C. A., DeFord, D. E., Bryk, A. S., & Seltzer, M. (1994). Comparing instructional models for the literacy education of high-risk first graders. *Reading Research Quarterly, 29,* 9-40.

Pinnell, G. S., Short, A. G., Lyons, C. A., & Young, P. (1986). *The Reading Recovery project in Columbus, OH, Year I: 1985-1986.* Columbus, OH: Ohio State University Press.

Profile Approach to Writing. (1995). *Profile Approach to Writing: Submission to the Program Effectiveness Panel of the U.S. Department of Education.* Washington, DC: U.S. Department of Education.

Project SEED, Inc. (1995). *Project SEED: Submission to the program effectiveness panel of the U.S. Department of Education.* Berkeley, CA & Dallas, TX: Author.

Puma, M. J., Karweit, N., Price, C., Ricciuti, A., Thompson, W., & Vaden-Kiernan, M. (1997). *Prospects: Final report on student outcomes.* Cambridge, MA: Abt Associates.

Quellmalz, E. S. (1987). Developing reasoning skills. In J. R. Baron, & R. J. Sternberg (Eds.), *Teaching thinking skills: Theory and practice.* New York: Fremman Press.

Quellmalz, E. S., & Hoskyn, J. A. (1988). Making a difference in Arkansas: The Multicultural Reading and Thinking Project. *Educational Leadership, 45*(7), 52-55.

Reid, E. M. (1989). *Exemplary Center for Reading Instruction: Submission to the Program Effectiveness Panel of the U.S Department of Education.* Washington, DC: U.S. Department of Education.

Rogers, M. R. (1993). *Increasing prevention of school failure by early intervention for school success of at-risk students kindergarten through grade three.* Practicum report, Nova University, Fort Lauderdale, FL.

Rosenshine, B., & Meister, C. (1994). Reciprocal teaching: A review of the research. *Review of Educational Research, 64*, 479-530.

Ross, S. M., Henry, D., Phillipsen, L., Evans, K., Smith, L., & Buggey, T. (1997). Matching restructuring programs to schools: Selection, negotiation, and preparation. *School Effectiveness and School Improvement, 8*, 36-65.

Ross, S. M., Smith, L. J., Casey, J., & Slavin, R. E. (1995). Increasing the success of disadvantaged children: An examination of alternative early intervention programs. *American Educational Research Journal, 32*, 773-899.

Rossi, R. J. (1996). *Evaluation of projects funded by the School Dropout Demonstration Assistance Program: Final evaluation report, Vol. I: Findings and recommendations*. Washington, DC: U.S. Department of Education.

Rothman, R. (1996). Reform at all levels: National alliance for restructuring education. In S. Stringfield, S. Ross, & L. Smith (Eds.), *Bold plans for school restructuring: The New American Schools Development Corporation Designs*. Mahwah, NJ: Erlbaum.

Rumberger, R. W. (1987). High school dropouts: A review of issues and evidence. *Review of Educational Research, 57*, 101-127.

Rumberger, R. W., & Larson, K. A. (1994). Keeping high-risk Chicano students in school: Lessons from a Los Angeles middle school dropout prevention program. In R. Rossi (Ed.), *Schools and students at risk*. New York: Teachers College Press.

Schaedel, B., Hertz-Lazarowitz, R., Walk, A., Lerner, M., Juberan, S., & Sarid, M. (1996). The Israeli CIRC (ALASH): First-year achievements in reading and comprehension. *Helkat-Lashon (Journal of Linguistic Education, 23*, 401-423, in Hebrew).

Schaffer, E. C., Nesselrodt, P. S., & Stringfield, S. C. (1997). *Impediments to reform: An analysis of destabilization issues in ten promising programs*. Arlington, VA: Educational Research Service.

Schubnell, G. O. (1996). Hawthorne Elementary School: The evaluator's perspective. *Journal of Education for Students Placed at Risk, 1* (1), 33-40.

Schweinhart, L. J., Barnes, H. V., & Weikart, D. P., with Barnett, W. S., & Epstein, A. S. (1993). *Significant benefits: The High/Scope Perry Preschool Study through age 27* (Monographs of the High/Scope Educational Research Foundation, 10). Ypsilanti, MI: High/Scope Press.

Schweinhart, L. J., & Weikart, D. P. (1980). *Young children grow up: The effects of the Perry Preschool program on youths through age 15*. Ypsilanti, MI: High/Scope Educational Research Foundation.

Schweinhart, L. J., Weikart, D. P., & Larner, M. B. (1986a). Child-initiated activities in early childhood programs may help prevent delinquency. *Early Childhood Research Quarterly, 1,* 303-312.

Schweinhart, L. J., Weikart, D. P., & Larner, M. B. (1986b). Consequences of three preschool curriculum models through age 15. *Early Childhood Research Quarterly, 1,* 15-45.

SCORE. (1994). Proposal submitted to the Program Effectiveness Panel of the United States Department of Education. Washington, D.C.: U.S. Department of Education.

Shanahan, T., & Barr, R. (1995). *Reading Recovery: An independent evaluation of an early instructional intervention for at-risk learners.* Chicago: University of Illinois at Chicago.

Sharan, S., & Shachar, H. (1988). *Language and learning in the cooperative classroom.* New York: Springer.

Sharan, Y., & Sharan, S. (1992). *Expanding cooperative learning through group investigation.* New York: Teachers College Press.

Sikorski, M. F., Wallace, T., Stariha, W. E., & Rankin, V. E. (1993). School reform and the curriculum. *New Directions for Program Evaluation, 59,* 1-37.

Sinclair, M., Thurlow, M., Christenson, S., & Evelo, D. (1995). Check and Connect Partnership for School Success: Project evaluation, 1990-1995. In U.S. Department of Education, *Staying in school: The ABC dropout prevention and intervention series.* Washington, DC: Author.

Sizer, T. (1984). *Horace's compromise: The dilemma of the American high school.* Boston: Houghton Mifflin.

Sizer, T. (1992). *Horace's school.* New York: Houghton Mifflin.

Sizer, T. (1996). *Horace's hope.* New York: Houghton Mifflin.

Skills Reinforcement Project. (1984). *Developing mathematical talent in minority and disadvantaged students.* Baltimore: Johns Hopkins University, Center for Talented Youth.

Skills reinforcement project. (1992). Proposal submitted to the Program Effectiveness Panel of the National Diffusion Network. Washington, DC: U.S. Department of Education.

Skills Reinforcement Project. (1995). *Evaluation report.* Baltimore: Johns Hopkins University, Center for Talented Youth.

Slavin, R. E. (1994). *Using student team learning* (4th ed.). Baltimore: Johns Hopkins University, Center for Social Organization of Schools.

Slavin, R. E. (1995). *Cooperative learning: Theory, research, and practice* (2nd ed.). Boston: Allyn & Bacon.

Slavin, R. E. (1997). Design competitions: A proposal for a new federal role in educational research and development. *Educational Researcher, 26*(1), 22-28.

Slavin, R. E., & Madden, N. A. (1991). Modifying Chapter 1 program improvement guidelines to reward appropriate practices. *Educational Evaluation and Policy Analysis, 13,* 369-379.

Slavin, R. E., & Madden, N. A. (1995, April). *Effects of Success for All on the achievement of English language learners.* Paper presented at the annual meeting of the American Educational Research Association, San Francisco.

Slavin, R. E., Madden, N. A., Dolan, L. J., & Wasik, B. A. (1994). Roots and Wings: Inspiring academic excellence. *Educational Leadership, 52*(3), 10-13.

Slavin, R. E., Madden, N. A., Dolan, L. J., & Wasik, B. A. (1996). *Every child, every school: Success for All.* Thousand Oaks, CA: Corwin.

Slavin, R. E., Madden, N. A., Dolan, L. J. Wasik, B. A., Ross, S., Smith, L., & Dianda, M. (1996). Success for All: A summary of research. *Journal of Education for Students Placed at Risk, 1,* 41-76.

Slavin, R. E., Madden, N. A., & Wasik, B. A. (1996). Roots and Wings. In S. Stringfield, S. Ross, & L. Smith (Eds.), *Bold plans for school restructuring: The New American Schools Development Corporation Designs.* Mahwah, NJ: Erlbaum.

Smith, L. J., Ross, S. M., & Casey, J. P. (1994). *Special education analyses for Success for All in four cities.* Memphis, TN: University of Memphis, Center for Research in Educational Policy.

Smith, M., & O'Day, J. (1991). Systemic school reform. In S. Fuhrman & B. Malen (Eds.), *The politics of curriculum and testing* (pp. 233-267). Bristol, PA: Falmer.

Stein, M. K., Leinhardt, G., & Bickel, W. (1989). Instructional issues for teaching students at risk. In R. E. Slavin, N. L. Karweit, & N. A. Madden (Eds.), *Effective programs for students at risk.* Boston: Allyn & Bacon.

Stern, D., Paik, I., Catterall, J. S., & Nakata, Y. (1989). Labor market experience of teenagers with and without high school diplomas. *Economics of Education Review, 8,* 233-246.

Stevens, R. J., & Durkin, S. (1992). *Using student team reading and student team writing in middle schools: Two evaluations* (Report No. 36). Baltimore: Johns Hopkins University, Center for Research on Effective Schooling for Disadvantaged Students.

Stevens, R. J., Madden, N. A., Slavin, R. E., & Farnish, A. M. (1987). Cooperative integrated reading and composition: Two field experiments. *Reading Research Quarterly, 22,* 433-454.

Stevens, R. J., & Slavin, R. E. (1995). Effects of a cooperative approach in reading and writing on academically handicapped and nonhandicapped students. *The Elementary School Journal, 95*(3), 241-262.

Stevenson, B. J. (1982). *An analysis of the relationship of student-student consultation to academic performance in differential classroom settings.* Unpublished doctoral dissertation, Stanford University.

Stringfield, S., Datnow, A., Herman, R., & Berkeley, C. (1997). Introduction to the Memphis restructuring initiative. *School Effectiveness and School Improvement, 8,* 3-35.

Stringfield, S., & McHugh, B. (1997). *The Maryland Core Knowledge implementation: First-year evaluation.* Baltimore: Johns Hopkins University, Center for Social Organization of Schools.

Stringfield, S., Millsap, M., & Herman, R. (1997). *Special strategies for educating disadvantaged children: Results and policy implications.* Washington, DC: U.S. Department of Education.

Stringfield, S., & Ross, S. M. (1997). A "reflection" at mile three of a marathon : The Memphis restructuring initiative in mid-stride. *School Effectiveness and School Improvement, 8,* 151-161.

Stringfield, S., Ross, S., & Smith, L. (Eds.). (1996). *Bold plans for school restructuring: The New American Schools Development Corporation Designs.* Mahwah, NJ: Erlbaum.

Swanson, M. C., Mehan, H., Hubbard, L. (1995). The AVID classroom: Academic and social support for low-achieving students. In J. Oakes & K. H. Quartz (Eds.), *Creating new educational communities. Ninety-fourth yearbook of the National Society for the Study of Education, Part I.* Chicago: University of Chicago Press.

Tomblin, E. A., & Davis, B. R. (1985). *Technical report of the evaluation of the race/human relations program: A study of cooperative learning environment strategies.* San Diego, CA: San Diego City Schools.

U.S. Department of Education. (1997). *The condition of education: 1997.* Washington, DC: Author.

Villaseñor, J.R.A., & Kepner, H. S. (1993). Arithmetic from a problem-solving perspective: An urban implementation. *American Educational Research Journal, 21*(1), 62-69.

Wallace, T. (1993). Chicago public schools: Evaluation of the 1987-88 Paideia program. In D. R. Waldrip, W. L. Marks, & N. Estes (Eds.), *Magnet school policy studies and evaluations* (pp. 477-515). Houston, TX: International Research Institute on Educational Choice.

Wasik, B. A. (1997). *Volunteer tutoring programs: A review of achieve-ment outcomes.* Baltimore: Johns Hopkins University, Center for Research on the Education of Students Placed at Risk.

Wasik, B. A., & Slavin, R. E. (1993). Preventing early reading failure with one-to-one tutoring: A review of five programs. *Reading Research Quarterly, 28,* 178-200.

Webster, W. J. (1995). *Executive summary: The evaluation of Project SEED 1991-1994.* Detroit, MI: Detroit Public Schools.

Webster, W. J., & Chadbourn, R. A. (1992). *The evaluation of Project SEED.* Dallas, TX: Dallas Independent School District.

Webster, W. J., & Russell, A. C. (1992). *Evaluation of Project SEED.* Dallas, TX: Dallas Independent School District.

Weikart, D. P., Rogers, L., Adcock, C., & McClelland, D. (1971). *The cognitively oriented curriculum: A framework for preschool teachers.* Urbana: University of Illinois.

Wells, J. (1981). SCORE. *Final report presented for ESEA Title IVC.* Sacramento: California Department of Education.

Ziegler, S. (1981). The effectiveness of cooperative learning teams for increasing cross-ethnic friendship: Additional evidence. *Human Organization, 40*(3), 264-268.

Zigler, E., Finn-Stevenson, M., & Linkins, K. W. (1992). Meeting the needs of children and families with Schools of the 21st Century. *Yale Law and Policy Review, 10* (1), 69-81.

Zigler, E., & Muenchow, S. (1992). *Head Start: The inside story of America's most successful educational experiment.* New York: Basic Books.

Zigler, E., & Valentine, J. (Eds.). (1973). *Project Head Start: A legacy of the War on Poverty.* New York: Free Press.

CORWIN
PRESS

The Corwin Press logo—a raven striding across an open book—represents the happy union of courage and learning. We are a professional-level publisher of books and journals for K–12 educators, and we are committed to creating and providing resources that embody these qualities. Corwin's motto is "Success for All Learners."